CLEARING
EMOTIONAL
CLUTTER

Praise for *Clearing Emotional Clutter*

"You cannot optimize your performance unless you can focus clearly. If negative thoughts or lack of self-esteem is holding you back, *Clearing Emotional Clutter* can help you unlock the key to yourself. You will see yourself more clearly. Better yet, you will be able to focus your attention and your abilities on your work with newfound clarity. Donald Altman provides simple-to-follow but powerful-to-use techniques that will enable you to optimize your abilities and leave your emotional baggage behind."

— **John Baldoni,** author of *Moxie* and *Lead by Example*

"*Clearing Emotional Clutter* shows how to banish old hurts and family pain that can weigh you down and block you from reaching your personal and professional goals. Donald Altman's de-cluttering lifestyle tools have the potential to rewire your brain so you can gain new levels of mental clarity, overcome limiting fears, enhance your relationships, and even untie knots of new emotional clutter in the moment. *Clearing Emotional Clutter* shows how to break the chains of the past and live in this moment in a more creative, adaptive, and spacious way."

— **Jeffrey M. Schwartz, MD,** author of *You Are Not Your Brain*

Praise for Donald Altman's *One-Minute Mindfulness*

"*One-Minute Mindfulness* is loaded with wisdom and includes practical exercises for tapping into the power of the here and now. Mindfulness is much more than just a spiritual practice. It awakens us to the joy of life. In the present moment, the whole world sparkles with beauty."

— **Tobin Blake,** author of *The Power of Stillness*

"Too much of the time we're running on automatic. In *One-Minute Mindfulness*, Donald Altman gently guides our focus of attention in directions that wake up the senses, nurture the soul, and uplift the spirit — in just sixty seconds! This book helps us make each new minute a potential encounter with life itself; the world very much needs this pragmatic spiritual book...right now."

— **John Selby,** author of *Quiet Your Mind* and *Expand This Moment*

"Engage your heart. Engage your mind. Engage your spirit. You have heard all this before, but now Donald Altman can show you how in *One-Minute Mindfulness*. This book is chock-full of insightful nuggets that will stimulate your mind and stir your heart."
— **John Baldoni,** author of *Lead with Purpose*

Praise for Donald Altman's *The Mindfulness Code*

"*The Mindfulness Code* can greatly enhance the ability of anyone to live with a greater sense of direction and self-control."
— **Jeffrey M. Schwartz, MD,** coauthor of *The Mind & the Brain*

"An antidote to the stress and hurriedness of modern life. In an age where we are pushed to perform ever better, Donald Altman reminds us that kindness, acceptance, and listening — just listening — are as admirable and transformative as any work or monetary achievement."
— **Robert Biswas-Diener,** coauthor of *Happiness*

"This well-written book addresses the root problems in anybody's life, and Altman's suggestions will certainly prove beneficial to readers who follow them."
— **Bhante Henepola Gunaratana,** author of
Mindfulness in Plain English

"*The Mindfulness Code* is a wonderful mix of warmth, humor, and gentle wisdom. Donald Altman weaves an engrossing blend of insights and personal stories from his many years as a skilled therapist along with illustrative research findings and many helpful mindfulness exercises. This book will hand you the keys for unlocking a life of greater ease and happiness."
— **Zen Roshi Jan Chozen Bays, MD,** author of
Mindful Eating and *A Year of Mindful Living*

CLEARING EMOTIONAL CLUTTER

*Mindfulness Practices
for Letting Go of What's Blocking
Your Fulfillment and Transformation*

DONALD ALTMAN

New World Library
Novato, California

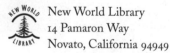

New World Library
14 Pamaron Way
Novato, California 94949

Text design by Tona Pearce Myers

Library of Congress Cataloging-in-Publication Data is available.

First printing, March 2016
ISBN 978-1-60868-364-2
EISBN 978-1-60868-365-9
Printed in Canada on 100% postconsumer-waste recycled paper

New World Library is proud to be a Gold Certified Environmentally Responsible Publisher. Publisher certification awarded by Green Press Initiative. www.greenpressinitiative.org

10   9   8   7   6   5   4   3   2   1

*This book is dedicated to all who courageously walk
the compassionate, peaceful, and humble path of mindfulness.
May all beings awaken and heal together.*

✦

CONTENTS

PART 3: PREVENTING NEW EMOTIONAL CLUTTER WITH DAILY DE-CLUTTERING

PART 4: TRANSFORMATION AND FULFILLMENT WITH PEACE, PURPOSE, AND WHOLENESS

INTRODUCTION

Don't own so much clutter that you will
be relieved to see your house catch fire.

— Wendell Berry, *Farming*

It's no surprise that emotional clutter from our past can stick to us like Super Glue to such an extent that we often consider it inseparable from our sense of self and personal identity. What may surprise you, though, is how easy-to-use daily practices can dissolve away all that toxic, sticky, clinging clutter — whether it is old emotional wreckage from your childhood or new emotional clutter that you take on every day.

What is emotional clutter? Emotional clutter could be an old childhood experience of being rejected by others, which may convince us we aren't really lovable. It could be an old family wound that still cuts deep. Or it could be an insensitive statement from a high school English teacher who once looked you straight in the eye and told you, "You can't make an 'A' student out of a 'B' student."

This last instance of unkind emotional clutter happened to me! Thankfully, I had other wonderfully supportive English teachers, and I didn't let this personal emotional clutter stick to me, though I was stunned and saddened by the comment at the time.

In fact, the cutting-edge science of epigenetics — which we'll explore in part 1 — shows that emotional clutter affects us at the cellular level, turning on and off genes related to our immune system and aging. It even suggests that painful emotional clutter may travel across generations. As shocking as that seems, it means we may be adversely affected by ancient family or cultural injustices, such as codependency, slavery, war, or the Holocaust.

One thing is certain: we all carry around some form of emotional clutter, baggage, trauma, adversity, or pain from the past. Whether the adversity is the result of what others have done to us or what we have done to others — or even the harm we have done to ourselves — the result is clear. *Old emotional clutter directly affects our ability to regulate emotions, experience joy, and have a fulfilling life. It even affects our physical well-being by putting the brakes on the immune system.*

Emotional clutter from the past is like old boxes of emotional stuff that fill up the attic of our minds. If what's in the attic leaves us feeling perpetually powerless, defensive, betrayed, sad, and unhappy, it can block us from recognizing the good and decent things in life. By contrast, the ability to be healthy, happy, and well balanced — and to live a meaningful and fulfilling life — could be defined by how well we clear out this attic. To do this we need to recognize, adapt, buffer, and regulate all the emotional junk that threatens to derail our goals and dreams.

To illustrate the sticking power of old emotional clutter, let me share the story of one of my clients, Margo (in this book, all names and identifying details of clients have been altered). A nicely dressed woman in her fifties, Margo came to see me for acute clinical depression. The attic of her mind was so crammed with old boxes of family-related emotional clutter that her ability to experience the here and now was severely limited. During my initial intake session, Margo kept returning to a particular box in her attic. She kept repeating a refrain that had become almost like a spiritual mantra. "My father, he abused me," she said, almost robotically. "He mistreated me. He said the most horrible things to me from the age of six."

Since this was our first session, I wanted to get more information about her life before exploring any specific issue. After empathizing with Margo, I tried to redirect her, but she was so fixed on the old story that she couldn't get free of it — like a car whose tires are caught in a deep, muddy rut. Finally, I said, "Margo, I notice that you keep returning to the story of you and your father, and I want to hear more about it at some point. But I'm curious — have you ever counted the number of times you tell yourself that story in the course of a day?"

Margo paused and put her hand up to her chin. She looked at me directly, as if she had just emerged from a deep trance (which indeed she had). "Funny you should ask me that. I *have* tried to count the number of times," she said, nodding her head, "but I always lose track. But I do know that when I don't tell myself that story, I'm a lot happier."

In another sense, Margo's unresolved emotional history was like a heavy, unwieldy bundle of emotional knots that she pulled along behind her each day. This knotted up history pulled her out of the present moment and kept her from living a joyful life and engaging in healthy relationships. Or you could compare this emotional debt to a dirty window through which she perceived daily events — because the window was smudged and dirty, it acted as a filter that blocked out the light. Sadly, she could never really see things as they were.

Interestingly, Margo was using a form of mantra, a potent awareness practice that we will explore in this book. However, Margo was using mantra in a negative way to hold her emotional blockage in place rather than using it to clear away clutter. As you will discover, positive affirmations and mantras are an effective method of using mindfulness to shift attention away from stuck and habitual ways of thinking.

In addition to clearing out old emotional clutter, we also must clear away *all the new clutter* that keeps trying to cling to us. It's similar to how tartar builds up on your teeth: accumulating new emotional clutter is a natural process, and it never stops. For many of us, though, being faced with new and seemingly never-ending clutter is frustrating and exasperating. If you think there are people who manage to avoid that clutter, think again. Not even Buddha could avoid emotional and mental clutter. However, the emotional clutter he encountered as a young man motivated him to find liberation from it — including the emotional clutter that arises in the moment due to craving and unhealthy desire.

What are the daily stresses that pull your life into chaos and create new emotional clutter? Real or even perceived danger in the environment can hijack the part of your brain that is focused on survival. The result? Your brain's emotional clutter processor — the amygdala, which we'll examine in chapter 2 — goes into overdrive. The pace of modern life and the number of things requiring our attention are probably greater today than at any time in all of history. We face information overload from email, news, the internet, and the increased complexity of living — such as the need to make decisions about insurance, school, transportation, health care, where to live, and how to pay for it all.

Concerns about major life transitions can create all kinds of emotional debris, too. One client, Richard, was constantly worried and anxious about his upcoming retirement. "I'm more prone to fear-based thinking than ever before in my life, and I don't know what to do about it," he lamented.

It's not just the big life transitions. Even making a small decision — such as where and how to buy a book — can require many choices: *Internet or retail store? Independent bookstore or chain? Price or convenience? Digital book or printed book? Standard shipping, two-day shipping, or overnight? Cash, PayPal, credit card, or debit card?* In fact, brain science tells us that the more choices you are forced to make during the day, the more your brain's energy gets sapped and depleted. It's no wonder that the never-ending small decisions of life can leave us feeling exhausted.

If your brain gets a constant download of emotional clutter from any of these sources, take a nice deep breath right now. That's because you're going to get an entirely different kind of brain download in this book — one that draws upon modern science and ancient practices and is designed to regulate your emotions, help you feel safe, and enrich your life.

If you want to manage your emotional clutter, the best place to begin is by managing your brain.

That's what we'll do in these pages.

A MINDFUL PATH FOR CLEARING EMOTIONAL CLUTTER

The purpose of *Clearing Emotional Clutter* is to help you heal and move on from pains, insults, traumas, toxic stressors, and emotional clutter from the past and the present — without blaming, shaming, or punishing yourself. I like to think of it as a *mindful lifestyle reboot* — a way of clearing out the old, habitual methods of living and thinking that keep us stuck in emotional clutter to the point that we can't imagine a way out. Most importantly, anyone can learn the skills needed to make this mindful lifestyle reboot, and it doesn't take a huge investment of time. Neuroscience tells us that even a few minutes a day can rewire the brain to clear unwanted emotional clutter from your life.

Clearing Emotional Clutter is organized in four parts. Part 1, "Recognizing and Clearing Away Old Emotional Clutter," examines how you can become more aware of the various kinds of old clutter that have negatively affected your life or disrupted your ability to get centered and emotionally regulated. It's like the first step in reprogramming your computer. If you don't recognize the harmful and habitual thought programs that are disrupting your brain's hard drive, how can you hope to fix the operating system? While your brain may have initially been shaped by conditions out of your control, the brain is extremely malleable. Neuroscience shows you can reshape the brain's inner architecture much like an athlete shapes her or his body by going to the gym. Through learning new tools, you become the master programmer capable of rewiring your brain.

In addition, you will learn effective mindfulness skills, or tools, for using your attention and present-moment focus to turn off these emotional clutter programs — in much the same way that you delete files or *empty the trash* in your hard drive. When you're in the moment, such as getting present in the body by becoming aware of your breath, you are running an entirely different program, one that is adaptive, is selective, and can dramatically transform your experience of life. In other words, you'll be "Inner-Facebooking" by paying attention to what cultivates your deepest inner sense of safety, values, fulfillment, and purpose.

Part 2, "Healing Relational, Cultural, and Ancestral Clutter," addresses significant relationships, family issues, and unhealthy cultural clutter. Because the brain is wired to relate to others, it's vital to clear out the clutter that prevents closeness, caring, and the feelings of safety and support that derive from healthy relationships. You'll practice communicating with others — and yourself — in a way that promotes trust and openness. You'll also discover the power of listening and learn why it can transform your experience of the emotional clutter that arises from those "difficult" persons in your life.

Part 3, "Preventing New Emotional Clutter with Daily Decluttering," explores a number of effective practices for preventing the buildup of *new* emotional muck. It offers tools for managing daily stress and transitions. During times of transition, we often experience uncertainty about what will happen next. This naturally produces feelings of anxiety and emotional clutter. This is true whether you're going through a major life transition — having a child, relocating, divorcing or breaking up, losing a job, or suffering health issues — or experiencing daily transitions, such as driving to an appointment or entering a workplace meeting. By incorporating into your lifestyle effective practices such as mindful grounding, connecting with nature, and simplifying your life, you will experience more joy each day while at the same time preventing the buildup of new emotional clutter.

Part 4, "Transformation and Fulfillment with Peace, Purpose, and Wholeness," takes you beyond emotional clutter to a more satisfying and meaningful place — your deeper life purpose. This is a gift where your life meaning and intention become as one. To that end, you will integrate into your lifestyle a capacity for softening the heart and healing ancient wounds, untying difficult knots — in the moment — before they bind you, and tapping into your wise self. This exploration can bring your most cherished values into the world in a truly self-sustaining and life-affirming way.

EXERCISING YOUR CLUTTER-CLEARING MINDFULNESS MUSCLES

Before embarking on your de-cluttering journey, here's a quick primer on the skills you'll be utilizing. You've likely heard the word *mindfulness* — but what does it really mean? How does mindfulness work? Throughout *Clearing Emotional Clutter*, you will directly apply the following skills, which are designed to clear out both old and new emotional clutter. I like to think of these as the Six Clutter-Clearing Mindfulness Skills, which can be easily understood and accessed through the acronym PAIR UP.

Anytime you feel overwhelmed by clutter, you can ask yourself the question, How can I better 'pair up' with what is happening right now? By tapping into each of these six key clutter sweepers, you can find emotional balance and harmoniously *pair up* with your surroundings in a way that brings purpose and clarity.

Here is what the acronym stands for:

P — Present-Moment Participation
A — Attuned Acceptance
I — Intentionality
R — Reflection

U — Understanding of Suffering
P — Purposeful Partnership

The first clutter-clearing skill is *Present-Moment Participation*. Too often, emotional clutter occurs when our minds wander off to the past or future. Mindfulness helps shift your attention away from thoughts of past trauma or persistent anxiety about the future by firmly anchoring your awareness in the here and now. Researchers from Harvard, in a study published in *Science*, studied how often people's minds wander, and they learned that our minds wander nearly half the time (about 47–48 percent). What is really interesting, however, is the finding that people are most happy when they are fully *participating* in the moment. In the study, mind wandering occurred most frequently when people were on the computer at work. People reported themselves as most present — and happy — when they were having a conversation, exercising, or engaged in sex. (Certainly, it's a good idea to be present during all these activities.)

Second, mindfulness cultivates a state of *Attuned Acceptance*. Through an attitude of acceptance we can better weather life's unexpected storms. Though many of us would like to believe that we're in control of what happens to us, life is often unpredictable and changing. Attuned acceptance means acknowledging honestly what is happening around us and with our inner feelings — allowing us to integrate and learn from even negative feelings and experiences. In addition, attunement with others allows us to sense what others are going through. With attunement we gain empathetic understanding as well as a sense of deep mutuality and reciprocal interaction with others. This helps us to be more authentic, harmonious, supportive, and understanding — vital building blocks that make for closer and more meaningful relationships.

The third clutter-clearing skill consists of *Intentionality*. Intentionality is about making our daily choices and actions — even the small ones — count. With intention, we can move through our day while minimizing new clutter and without mindlessly leaving messes behind that will need to be cleaned up later. Ethical choice-making invites a more heart-centered way of living that emphasizes service and compassionate living and is less focused on acquiring more stuff (yes, more clutter).

The fourth skill is *Reflection*, or the ability to look inwardly at our thoughts and emotions. This invites deep inquiry into the root causes of our emotional clutter. Investigation of this kind often produces insight, cultivates wisdom, and is self-regulating because we are examining our thoughts and emotions rather than letting them run amok. When we pause long enough, we can observe not only thoughts and emotions but especially desires and cravings, which always deserve a second look. If you have ever had an uncontrollable craving that has caused problems — such as binge eating — then you know how critical it can be to examine that craving instead of just reacting impulsively. With reflection, we can wisely choose to move our thoughts — and life — in an entirely new direction.

The fifth skill consists of *Understanding of Suffering*. If we don't really understand how emotional clutter sticks to us and comes into our lives, how can we ever hope to slow it down or stop it? By more clearly understanding the roots of suffering, we can pull out those weeds before they grow into massive, invasive vines that choke our growth. One such root is attaching or clinging to someone or something that is temporary — and not permanent and everlasting, as we would wish. We cannot hold on to anything for long — that lustrous paint on the new car gets chipped and eventually dulls. Our once-youthful bodies get old and wrinkled. As songwriter Leonard Cohen once wrote, "Well, my friends are gone, and my hair is grey. I ache in the places where I used to play." But this understanding is not meant to produce unhappy clutter. Rather, we become enriched as we notice the myriad causes of our own anguish. This has three beneficial effects. We pull up the negative roots causing us distress, we lighten up through recognition and acceptance, and perhaps most importantly, we grow in compassion for others who must inevitably experience loss, grief, and sorrow. Through understanding suffering, we increase our compassion, empathy, and universal kinship, and it softens our hearts and makes us more human. We can bring compassion into our words, hearts, and action.

The final mindfulness antidote for clearing clutter is *Purposeful Partnership*. This book ends by exploring how to transform our lives by bringing a central purpose into partnership with others and the world. Life purpose elevates our existence, even our daily experience, by bringing our deepest values into the forefront. It gives us a big picture view of what matters most. When integrated with enlightened partnership, purpose can blossom and grow into something we might never have imagined. Partnership acknowledges that all we do is in relationship to something else.

Whenever you use any of these mindfulness skills, you are actually practicing all of them. Each increases our awareness of what brings the clutter of pain and suffering as well as what brings joy and fulfillment. These six skills are like the engine under the hood of the car — out of sight but necessary to get us moving to our destination. Though not always directly referred to, these principles are embedded within, and integral to, the hands-on Lifestyle Tools I've included in this book. Whenever you need to, refer back to PAIR UP as your all-purpose reminder of how to get centered.

START WHERE YOU ARE

I remember once hearing a carnival barker say to a crowd, "Take one step forward, and your body will naturally follow!" What great advice for embarking on any journey. Just take that first step, which you have already done by reading these pages. While taking a carnival ride gets your adrenaline going, this journey is a gentle and forgiving path to healing from emotional clutter.

During most journeys it's all too easy to get wrapped up in how things will turn out. We may be tempted to rate the journey and judge ourselves on whether we succeed or fail. Letting go of expectation, however, gives us greater freedom to simply experience the journey itself, without being limited or hindered by our critical inner voices. *Trust that by getting into the process you will get to your destination.*

We are fortunate to live in a time when the teachings of our wisdom traditions are being affirmed by modern science, both of which tell us that we *can* make these critical shifts in awareness. As the ancient mystics long suspected, finding clarity, peace, and contentment is an inside job attained by using various meditative tools. We'll use these ancient tools to manage twenty-first-century emotional clutter.

Removing life's emotional clutter and finding fulfillment and contentment may not be easy, but it isn't an illusion. This is, perhaps, our greatest gift and innate human potential. All of us can do this, and we don't have to go into a cave and meditate. You can do this in your own backyard, so to speak, using the conditions that life has presented to you as your homework.

What better time and place to start than now?

∞

—— *Part 1* ——

RECOGNIZING AND CLEARING AWAY OLD EMOTIONAL CLUTTER

The body and mind act as a personal container through which awareness is either purified and cleansed or muddied and obscured by past, sticky emotional debris. In this section you will develop the skill of cleansing your awareness and emptying your container of old and persistent mental wounds and self-inflicted beliefs. To do this is to touch the heart of a profound and life-affirming transformation.

Chapter 1

STOP RIDING
THE EMOTIONAL ELEVATOR

Help me to love a slow progression,
to have no prejudice
that up is better than down or vice versa.
Help me to enjoy the in-between.

— Gunilla Norris, *Being Home*

Things go your way, you get that big promotion, you get that new house you always wanted, you have a happy thought about yourself, you get a nice compliment, and the elevator goes up.

Or things don't go your way, you get sick, your partner leaves you, you think you're inadequate, your friend ignores your text, and the elevator goes down.

Awakening is your ticket off the elevator ride. It's knowing what pushes the elevator buttons. With this amazing gift, you suddenly realize that the real prize is getting free from those buttons and not obsessively pressing them like a lab rat trying to get a reward or avoid a shock.

Yes, the elevator ride can be exhilarating. But it can be tiresome and exhausting, too. Are you ready to get off the elevator? If so, you are ready for this very special gift for transforming emotional rubble from the past. Being fully awake is a path to joy, to peace.

✦

The summer air hung heavy and moist inside the big hall where I sat with seventy-five other meditators during a silent ten-day retreat in upstate New York. My eyes were closed, and I'd been meditating for half an hour or more. I was aware of my breath moving in and out as my belly expanded and compressed. I had a sense of peace and calm. And then...

A loud, unexpected noise broke the silence like a crackle of thunder. Our guide, a Tibetan lama, clapped his hands together while loudly exclaiming a short, monosyllable that sounded something like "PEIIAY." After this initial jolt, he said in a staccato-like voice, "Who is doing the listening? Who is in there? Who is sitting? Who is meditating? Who and what are pushing your buttons and making you feel good or bad? Where's that voice that's commenting on it all? Who? What? Where?"

The lama's questions pierced my consciousness like a lightning bolt. Where exactly *was* this person I'd come to identify myself with? Was there really anybody in there? Where was that voice in my head coming from — the one that didn't exactly sound like my real voice? The one that never seemed to want to shut up and was always looking for attention and validation — which was one reason why I was meditating.

For a moment the wheels in my head stopped spinning. They simply could not compute the lama's impenetrable questions. For a brief gap, maybe in exasperation, the mind shut down and all that was left was awareness. The ego's committee of voices that ceaselessly spins talk and tales had ceased. There was no longer a "me" in the way. Just spacious awareness. Just this. Just the gap. Just presence.

✦

The lama's queries might seem like odd ones to entertain. Especially living in a culture — no, a world — where having a strong personality gets you on TV, where individual initiative and creativity are highly sought-after qualities, and where constant stimulation makes contemplation and looking inward less understood, if not actively avoided.

In fact, a study conducted by psychologists at the University of Virginia and Harvard University and published in the journal *Science* indicates that people are quite unwilling to sit with their thoughts. Asked to be alone with their thoughts for six to fifteen minutes in a closed room in a lab or at home, from one-third to one-half of the participants cheated and listened to music or used their phone. In a later study, researchers placed subjects in a room where they could voluntarily self-administer an electric shock to themselves rather than be alone with their thoughts. Over half gave themselves shocks.

Is being present without some form of stimulation really so scary? What would you do given this choice? What *do* you do when you are alone? If you fear the unwanted scenarios your mind can conjure up when left to its own devices, that's perfectly understandable. To verify our mind's ability to scare the hell out of us, researchers tested university students in thirteen different countries and six different continents. The results, published in the *Journal of Obsessive-Compulsive and Related Disorders*, found that 94 percent of participants had experienced an unwanted thought in the previous three months — usually some form of intrusive doubt. A lesser number experienced some kind of repugnant intrusive thought. This is why I often write the following words on the whiteboard in my office:

Thoughts are not necessarily facts.
Most of the time they're not even close.

Imagine, for a moment, that you're sitting on a beautiful sand beach in Malibu when you suddenly have the most anxious, worrisome thought in the world. Other than a few tanned Californians with towels, there's absolutely nothing dangerous on that beach. And yet a scary thought can produce a powerful effect — hijacking the joy and experience of that moment.

On the other hand, what if you simply observed the same thought as nothing more than a mental sensation? In other words, suppose you viewed it as no different than a physical sensation — except that it's happening in the mind? A physical sensation is not you, is it? It's a momentary, fleeting feeling in the body. Likewise, a mental sensation isn't you. Thoughts are a natural process, and it means your brain is working, which is a good thing. What's not helpful is when habitually anxious or ruminating thoughts and cravings — the debris from past emotional wreckage — hijack your brain from your present-moment experience.

Rather than go to war with your thoughts by fighting them or fearing them, you can take a more diplomatic, or detached, approach by engaging mindfulness. To better understand this idea, I interviewed Paul Harrison, a longtime meditator and the director of *The Mindfulness Movie*. He said he underwent a major shift in awareness that dramatically changed his life:

> I had an experience at a young age where I understood that I was not the ego. It happened one afternoon. As I was sitting at my desk feeling extremely frustrated with my meditation practice, I noticed the lemon tree outside my window. I began staring at one of the lemons until I completely lost awareness of myself. I was so absorbed in the lemon that I wasn't aware of time or of my surroundings. Then there was an instant shift of perception, and I understood that the source of thought — that moment

before a thought actually occurs in the mind — was actually emptiness. It was an empty awareness that was alive and full and permeated the emptiness of the universe. And finally, I realized that the "I" was simply a tool that the mind produces. We think we need it. But there is something much deeper within us all.

That one change in perspective has stayed with me throughout my whole life and has kept me grounded. I used to be motivated by money, but I know now that money is also a tool. That change of perspective helped balance my life, and because of that I spent more time with my kids when they were young and needed me most, and I know that enjoying quality time in my life is worth more to me than the typical things many people spend so much time acquiring.

Since that experience, I've never been prone to depressive tendencies. It goes back to that inner knowing that a state of sadness is just passing through the mind. There is a detached state of awareness that remains objective to the sadness. That's not to say that I don't get out of balance! But it gives me an overall perspective that I need to start shifting back to my balance state. The universe becomes aware of itself through your body and mind, and when you realize it — that's the gift.

TO WAKE UP, SEE BEYOND THE HIJACKER

Your birthright is spacious awareness — a powerful presence that is empty of worry, guilt, and fear. Take a moment to imagine what that would be or feel like. It's like noticing our mental states from a safe distance. As Paul's story demonstrates, one way to get off the elevator ride is to not be so attached to, or hijacked by, the

"I-centric" point of view — what I like to think of as the "I, me, my, and mine."

Suppose, for example, that you toss a bucket of red paint into the air. Is the air colored or tainted by the paint? No, it hasn't changed. It's still just the air. Spacious awareness is like that — it is untainted by our egocentric "I" thoughts about events that come and go. Your thoughts are like that spattering paint that doesn't really stick to the air.

By cultivating spacious awareness you can slowly detach from the limiting filters of "I, me, my, and mine" — thus loosening your identification with the never-ending stream of thoughts that can keep you tight, on edge, and reactive. This bare awareness doesn't take sides — it's not adding anything to your experience or subtracting anything from it. It's not judging the thoughts or defining who you are because of the mind's content. Awareness simply observes without an agenda, other than to let you be aware, present, and at rest.

LIFESTYLE TOOL: Stop Riding the Elevator Meditation

There's no special equipment to buy to get off the emotional elevator and cultivate spacious awareness. Stepping off the elevator is a process of letting the mind settle down and coming into the body's presence. This Lifestyle Tool helps you do this in three easy steps. To begin, find a natural setting where you will not be interrupted for five or ten minutes. (Shocking yourself is optional.) Any natural setting will do: a park, a courtyard with one tree or shrub, or a small yard with a few blades of grass. A sky with clouds is always nice; it's a way to throw your gaze far, far out.

1. See if your mind can empty itself in the sky and clouds. See if, for just a second, you can get lost in a tree's mass of leaves and branches. Notice how, even for a split

second, in that moment between thoughts the "I" fades away. There is just the observer, just awareness. Just space *between* the thoughts. This is the bigger you, without boundaries. How wonderful!

2.   It doesn't matter if you have lots on your mind. Don't wait until you finish chores or work or other tasks. In fact, it's better that you stop in the middle of those mental demands to do this. You'll notice the mind's resistance to sitting and noticing. As you sit, simply witness what the mind does, how it reacts, comments, advertises, distracts, fills with desire, craves, avoids, wants to take the body elsewhere, erupts in intrusive thoughts, and so on. What a great show! Don't fight anything. You might even comment, "Hello, again, mind. Thank you for these thoughts," before returning to nature. If you feel emotions, notice what they are and where you sense them in the body. Eventually (although "eventually" is relative), the mind will get the idea that you're not going to fight with it and that this game is no fun.

3.   No matter how often the mind intrudes, remember to breathe. Exhale slowly. Then bring your gaze back to nature. There's no limit to how long or when you can do this training. Try it at lunch for a minute or at home for an hour in the backyard. Afterward, when you are done, sit with the following questions. I recommend actually writing down your answers in a journal that you can refer back to as you go through this book.

•   How did your thinking, analyzing, critical mind get in the way? How did you manage to let it go, not resist it, and get beyond it? How does the internal committee of "I, me, my, and mine" color your daily experiences?

- What was it like to just witness thoughts — as opposed to react to them?
- How would you describe those moments when you were empty of the "I" viewpoint? Can you recall a time in your life when you experienced this?
- How can you use this practice to get grounded when your emotional buttons — both the up and down ones — are being pushed?

Invite self-compassion and patience as you use any of this book's Lifestyle Tools. No one is ever "perfect" when it comes to learning about the nature of the mind, and so you get an A+ for trying. Remember, too, that you're not trying to stop thoughts. Rather, you're making friends with the mind, marveling at how it works, and getting off the emotional elevator through cultivating spacious awareness and identifying less with your mental merry-go-round.

∞

Chapter 2

INNER-FACEBOOKING

What if you could erase everybody's memory of how the world operates? In that moment, the world would be born anew.
                                        — John Nelson, *Matrix of the Gods*

Are you an avid social networker? How does your time on Facebook or other social networking sites usually make you feel? Do you notice when your mood goes up or down? Do you notice the streams of memories, thoughts, or desires that get stimulated by the images and posts of others? Many people use social networking in a positive way to stay in touch with distant friends and family. In the same way, we need to constantly stay in touch with the "posts" we're putting up in our own minds, as well as the instant "texting" sent to us by the body — all of which I like to think of as *Inner-Facebooking*.

Inner-Facebooking skills are all about how you use one of your most precious resources: *your attention*. Your attention is what you use here and now to navigate your world. While others may try to grab your attention for their own purposes, no one other than you, ultimately, can decide how to use and harness this gift of awareness.

To illustrate what I mean, take the following brief survey:

- In what ways have you used your attention today?
- How often did technology grab your attention?
- How good do you feel about where you placed your attention?
- Did you use attention to help you feel more balanced and at peace?

Attention is necessary to regulate your emotions and help you maintain your emotional equilibrium throughout your day. By Inner-Facebooking, you can be more aware of harmful or distracting external or internal "posts." You notice the subtle signals of tightness, stress, or dis-ease your body is sending you. Knowing how to shift your attention lets you become skillful at putting up nurturing, feel-good posts that get you motivated, inspired, and involved. With Inner-Facebooking, you become proficient at noticing your moods, sensing emotions in your body, and cultivating the attitude of an impartial observer as you rebalance in the moment. To do this is to literally rewire and reshape how your brain makes connections.

On the other hand, if you lack Inner-Facebooking skills, you might find yourself hopelessly mired in negative clutter from the past. In one of the biggest studies of its kind in the United Kingdom, researchers analyzed more than thirty-two thousand participants who completed an online survey related to stress and repetitive, self-defeating thoughts. While the study determined that traumatic life events and family history were the largest predictors of depression and anxiety, there was one vital variable that kept stress in check. That mediating variable was one's *perception* of stress. If you strongly believe that you can't cope with a stressful situation, then you won't. However, if you shift your attention so as to view the situation from a distance, you can think about it and assess it differently. You might say, "Yes, this is stressful, but I've handled these kinds of situations effectively before. And I can find resources to help me get through it successfully." As Professor Peter Kinderman, lead researcher of the UK study, said, "Whilst we can't change a person's family history or their life experiences, it is possible to help a person to change the way they think and to teach them positive coping strategies that can mitigate and reduce stress levels."

WHERE'S YOUR ATTENTION RIGHT NOW?

Do you ever feel like the more you pay attention to your emotional wounds, the more you *continue* to pay attention to them? Preoccupation with negative past experiences may inadvertently hardwire the emotional clutter circuits in the brain. Imagine rolling a rock down a hill over the same path time and time again. Before long you create a groove or rut that guides the rock down the exact same path every time.

Our brain has the ability to create pathways, and change them, in much the same way through the process of neuroplasticity. When we think and behave in a certain way, the brain generates a pathway. Over time, frequently used pathways get wired together, creating an established path or groove. It's empowering to know that how we notice and respond to our thoughts can change the physical structure of the brain — even those habitually used emotional-clutter pathways.

Dr. Jeffrey Schwartz, author of *Brain Lock*, is a pioneer in neuroplasticity and repairing negative brain grooves. He developed a four-part mindfulness method for patients with obsessive-compulsive disorder (OCD). Instead of having patients take their repetitive and alarming thoughts at face value, Schwartz directs them to mentally *change their relationship* to those damaging thoughts. First, patients notice the old thoughts, and then they reappraise them in new ways. Before and after brain scans of patients have shown how their thinking can deactivate the OCD wiring in the brain by creating new neural pathways to replace the faulty ones. Patients learn how to harness the skill of Inner-Facebooking to notice and release their repetitive thoughts from the habitual groove.

Inner-Facebooking makes us aware of how we're using our attention and gives us some constructive distance from offending thoughts so we can decide how to respond to them. We can shift attention in a number of ways, including reflecting inwardly on that initial thought, finding a more realistic thought, or engaging in an action or behavior that reflects our deeper values.

Fred was a thirty-two-year-old client who, in my experience, lacked Inner-Facebooking skills. He was stuck in depression. I soon learned that when Fred was not working, he devoted all his free time to building a virtual life online as a vitriolic political blogger. The dark side of this blogging was that Fred so strongly identified with his political beliefs that he was consumed with anger. He was oblivious to the lighter side of life to such an extent that he developed what I fondly call ESD, or extreme seriousness disorder. As you might guess, Fred's ESD was fraying his relationship with his new girlfriend.

I also learned that Fred grew up in an authoritarian, adopted family and was told he would never amount to much. Fred's need to broadcast and impose inflexible views upon others was not unlike what he had experienced during his childhood with his rigid, self-righteous parents. It was very likely that Fred's mental grooves were ancient and deep. To counter ESD and his mental and emotional ruts, I had Fred try an experiment where he distanced himself from blogging every other day for a week. On nonblogging days he replaced blogging with other activities he enjoyed — hiking, walking, reading. I instructed him to practice Inner-Facebooking on the days he blogged, by noticing the emotional posts he was making in his mind and feeling in his body. Finally, I asked Fred to rate his mood from negative to positive on a scale of 1 to 10 each day for the week. I also asked Fred to practice noticing and naming his emotions — another important Inner-Facebooking technique.

J. David Creswell published research in *Psychosomatic Medicine* that demonstrates that, by naming our emotions as we experience them, we can more easily detach from that emotion and not automatically react to it. By shifting focus and making the emotion *the object of our attention*, we create a healthy distance from that emotion. We are no longer being pushed and pulled around by emotional baggage. We stop identifying with the powerful emotion and are more in control. Creswell's work shows that by naming our emotions we quiet down and inhibit the amygdala (described further below), a key part of the brain implicated in triggering emotional arousal and the body's ancient stress response.

A personal example of how this naming process has worked for me involves coping with "road rage." In the past, if a driver cut me off on the freeway, I often experienced a quick emotional reaction — followed by a few choice expletives. These negative emotions usually took a long time to dissipate. But the instant I *named my emotions* — a mixture of impatience, frustration, and superiority at being a "better" driver — I felt an immediate change. By taking a step back, I was no longer experiencing the emotions but was simply observing them with a sense of curiosity. This Inner-Facebooking also gave me a deeper understanding of my old habitual grooves, and it helped me be less reactive in the future. This is how Inner-Facebooking establishes a new brain pathway.

How did Inner-Facebooking work for Fred? He was surprised to discover that he was much happier, more curious, and more enthusiastic on those days he wasn't blogging. By Inner-Facebooking, he grew much more aware of how his blogging increased tension in his body and increased his negative thoughts and emotions.

While he remained committed to his beliefs and causes, Fred took a more neutral and relaxed stance toward blogging. He slowly let this activity go to spend time on other pursuits, including working as a volunteer to teach children about the environment. There isn't anything wrong with having strong political views, sharing your opinions, or writing political blogs. But ask yourself, do the ways you express and experience these views enhance your life or create clutter? It's like playing a sport — can you enjoy the game while accepting that you will lose some of the time? Or do you take losses and disagreements personally, letting them steal away the joy of the game? Do these feelings eat away at you long after the game (or the blog) is over? Fred learned to care without taking things so personally.

By Inner-Facebooking, Fred's physical health improved, too. Ruminating or anxious thoughts actually affect the body's immune functioning. Years ago, this might have been considered a New Age idea. Nowadays, a solid mountain of evidence shows that negative thoughts do indeed affect us at the cellular level, from upping the levels of cortisol in the body (which damages the immune system) to shortening our telomeres (which are biological markers of aging).

It's Not the Stress That Gets You

You've no doubt heard of the stress response. Knowing how to combat stress is critical because it can shut down the part of the brain's hard drive — the frontal cortex, located behind the forehead — that does our rational thinking. The Navy SEALs teach recruits a number of practices to keep their thinking brain online during dangerous missions. To understand this, it's important to know that when you encounter a threatening situation, a structure deep in the brain known as the amygdala sends out warning signals, releasing the hormones adrenaline and cortisol to prepare the body for danger. This protects you against a potential threat to your survival, like being attacked by a mugger or a dangerous animal. Just like the smoke detector in your house, the amygdala is always ready to sound the alarm.

This is an adaptive system, one designed to keep you alive. But what if a threat exists primarily in your mind — such as an anxious or fearful thought? Or what if a coworker or partner says something critical that makes you feel defensive? The brain's smoke detector doesn't know the difference! It still sounds the alarm, and when that happens, you can't just sit down and calmly talk it over or think about it. Powerful hormones have hijacked your rationality — as well as the thinking part of your brain. If this continues for two or more days, the cortisol in your body puts the brakes on your immune system by killing T cells and natural killer (NK) cells that fight infections and even some kinds of tumors. Studies have even shown that people who go to bed at night lonely or sad wake up in the morning with a higher cortisol load in the body. It's as if your body is tuning in to your experiences throughout the day and preparing you for stress.

While the brain gets wired to respond in certain ways after years of emotional conditioning, it's *how* you respond to emotional stress and clutter *the next time* that can make all the difference. The Inner-Facebooking Lifestyle Tool below will help you regulate your emotions more easily — whether to clear out old or new emotional clutter. With this skill, you will tune in to what's happening, lessen your stress in the moment, and bring your rational brain back online.

Inner-Facebooking is not the only Lifestyle Tool for working with stress in *Clearing Emotional Clutter*. As you try these different tools, find out which ones work best for you. In this way you can develop your own personal program for getting unstuck from emotional grooves. Remember, too, that you can always adapt any of these tools so they fit better with your lifestyle or complement how you like to learn.

This tool changes your fundamental relationship with emotional clutter. This exercise consists of two parts.

Part 1

First, recall an event related to your past emotional clutter that has stuck with you over the years — such as how others may have harmed you, rejected you, or held you back. Normally, you wouldn't want to practice remembering old clutter — which can reinforce it. Rather, the purpose here is to learn how to disconnect from it. By reexperiencing past emotional clutter, you can understand it better and recognize the signs for when you've drifted into this old rut or path. As you do this, if it ever feels too difficult, remind yourself that you are safe and that you can stop anytime you want.

Once you "connect" with your clutter, reflect on the following questions:

- Notice your body: What is your facial expression? Are you clenched up or tight in some way? Is your expression one of frowning or tightness?

- Notice your mood: How would you describe your emotional state while experiencing this clutter?
- If possible, name the emotions you feel — this is important because the process of naming creates distance and takes you out of the grip of the emotions. Is there sadness, anger, guilt, regret, disappointment, frustration, or another emotion? Don't name just one emotion — often several emotions are mixed together. Name as many as you can to accurately describe your feelings.
- Notice your energy level: Do you feel energetic and motivated, or do you feel heavy, weighed down, or immobilized?
- Finally, ask yourself these questions: How entangled am I with this clutter? How frequently do I think about it during the day? How does it affect the way I relate to others? How much of my energy is sapped and drained by it?

Part 2

Next, use the following two visualizations to shift your attention away from this remembered clutter. Think of these as your "clutter-free visualizations."

For the first visualization, take a nice deep breath and exhale slowly. This is known as belly breathing, and it gets air into the deepest part of the lungs and squeezes on the abdominal cavity, causing the belly to move outward. After breathing in as long as you can, filling your lungs and belly, exhale very slowly.

As you exhale, imagine that your out-breath is carrying the old emotional clutter, tightness, and tenseness down the body and letting it exit out the bottom of the feet. Take as many of these releasing breaths as you want, each time clearing away any remaining negative feelings as they exit the bottom of your feet and get deposited back into the earth for recycling. Usually, three to five breaths are good enough.

For the second clutter-free visualization, picture a time in your life when you felt lighter and more joyful — maybe at a favorite place or with a favorite person. Recall your experience in detail, noticing everything you love about that particular favorite place or person. Relish the favorite memory right now, letting yourself experience all the sights, sounds, and sensations. Let all the wondrous sensations and lightness of the experience seep into all the cells of your body. Let yourself relish in this feeling for up to five minutes.

Next, answer the following questions:

- How did the visualizations for turning away from clutter make you feel? What does your body feel like right now? What about your mood and energy levels? What is your facial expression?
- If you could, right now, untie the knots of old emotional debts, releasing them all, how would that make you feel, without that weight?
- What would your life be like without old emotional wounds taking up your time and energy?

Just trying out this Lifestyle Tool and considering these questions take courage and put you squarely on the clutter-removing path. In addition, you are putting to use one of the awareness practices in this book — dramatically shifting your present-moment focus — to clear away some of your old clutter so your Inner-Facebooking system can serve you in more positive and productive ways.

∞

Chapter 3

CULTIVATE A BEAUTIFUL GARDEN
OF THOUGHT

The flowers of positive experiences crowd out and gradually replace the
weeds of negative thoughts, feelings, and desires.
— Rick Hanson, *Hardwiring Happiness*

To create a beautiful garden, the gardener doesn't leave the grounds untended. Expert gardeners know that weeds will find a way to sneak into any space, so they are always on the lookout. Likewise, creating a beautiful garden in the mind doesn't happen without effort and skill. It requires constant tending of your thoughts — pulling out those negative weeds while watering and nurturing the seeds of thought that you want to grow and flourish. Buddhist teacher Lama Surya Das, a true *wise guy* (whom I call the Lama of Laughter) made this point with laser-like insight and a sense of humor when he said, "Practice being there while getting there."

How true. In the first two chapters, we have explored methods for getting off the emotional elevator by noticing the nature of the mind and what it easily attaches to. We have also rested the weary mind to quiet the busyness of our thinking and create some space around old clutter through Inner-Facebooking. Now let's start working on developing that garden of thought that only you can create.

NUTRIENTS FOR PLANTING
A GARDEN OF THOUGHT

When I first moved to Portland — which is nicknamed the Rose City — I figured it would be a snap to plant roses in my back-yard. Naïvely, I figured that I could stick them in the ground and they'd flourish. Seems I didn't consider the gophers, the deer, the rabbits, and all the other critters that couldn't wait to munch on the tender rose shoots and leaves. I learned to have patience, since it literally took years to nurture and grow those roses. I also dis-covered that because the soil in my backyard had a lot of clay — which acted as clutter that blocked growth — I had to bring in fresh soil that had the right nutrients.

Could your mind be too cluttered and lacking the proper nu-trients to grow a thriving garden? Reflect for a few moments on the following questions:

- How much of your day do you spend thinking about how others have harmed you or held you back?
- Do you constantly blame yourself for a failed relationship or think about the harm (intentional or unintentional) that you have done to others?
- How entangled are you with this emotional baggage?
- How much of your energy is sapped and drained by it?

It takes courage to consider these questions honestly. An-swering them means that you are willing to entertain a new di-rection — which is part of preparing your mind for new seeds of thought. It means admitting that things aren't always so black-and-white. It means that you are open enough not just to go with the status quo but to inquire deeply into your actions, thoughts, and intentions. In doing this you have taken an important first step — which is simply to acknowledge the effect your old emotional wounding has had on your life and your desire to change it.

Next, in order to prepare your mind with the right nutrients and soil for growth, ask yourself the following questions:

- What would it be like if you could discharge these emotional or psychic wounds — and really put them to rest?
- What if you could untie the knots of these old emotional debts? How would your life — in this very moment — be different?
- How ready are you to plant a new garden of thought and to let go of the old one?

We aren't always ready for a new garden. Why would someone decide to stay with an emotional wound rather than try to clear it up or cleanse it? For some individuals, oddly enough, suffering provides its own reason or rationale for being. The story of emotional pain can become part of one's identity. For example, I once worked at an eating disorder clinic, and several individuals spoke as if their eating disorder had become fused with their sense of self. More than one patient basically said, "Who would I be without my eating disorder?" So, too, we might ask, "Who would I be without my ruminating and anxious thoughts or my thoughts of victimization?"

There may be other reasons that we hold on to our emotional wounds. No one, including myself, is immune to anger and righteous indignation, which can come from witnessing or being subjected to an injustice or unfair treatment. Righteousness gives us the sense of being on the good, even moral side of things — which eases our doubts with a sense of certainty and clear absolutes. Anger can give us a feeling of power and control where before we might have had none. These emotions in themselves are not "wrong" — nor should we be unresponsive to injustices — but our attachment to these feelings can turn into invasive emotional weeds that can choke out healthy flowers and grass. In the bigger picture, the wiser view, we need to consider whether righteous indignation creates more suffering or less suffering. In other words, is our righteousness of service? Or is it self-serving and ego-driven in some regard?

Preparing our mental garden for planting is very much about our attachments — about how strongly attached we are to the emotional suffering, the harmful behaviors, and the selfish desires that ensnare us. Learning to let go of what does not serve us, or others, is one way of releasing the baggage we are holding on to. That's also one purpose of forgiveness, isn't it?

Congratulations on beginning the hard work of tilling the garden and preparing it for growth. You don't have to have all the answers. By asking the hard questions and looking within, you have begun the work. Now, let's plant some new seeds through the process of telling a story.

SCULPTING YOUR GARDEN
WITH STORIES OF STRENGTHS

Most mental gardens — whether they are filled with upsetting and disturbing weeds or soothing and nurturing flowers — consist of stories that describe our life and experiences. Right now, think about a vivid negative or positive memory. How would you describe it? Likely you would tell a story. Why is this so? Because the brain is wired for language and narrative. Many of our stories are not always accurate, since we learn storytelling styles and ways of interpreting events from our families and culture.

I wouldn't blame you if you were skeptical about the power of stories. It's fair to ask if stories really have this kind of power over our lives. Could the wrong stories lead us toward a life of high stress, failure, poor relationships, and unhappiness?

My experience working with Gary — a former drug addict and prison inmate — is one example of how our stories can help us to reimagine our lives. Hearing Gary's childhood story didn't really surprise me. It was riddled with abuse, chaos, and fear. His parents were drug users who were unreliable and emotionally out of control. As a result, Gary didn't trust relationships — and who could blame him?

Gary had come to me because he was failing miserably at the vocational training curriculum he was enrolled in — a program that was helping him realize his dream of getting a stable job. Gary had recently been released from prison, and going to school was a major, positive life direction for him. But it was going down the drain because his highly chaotic life and relationships were getting in the way — which mirrored what he had learned in childhood. He lived with his girlfriend in a home belonging to his partner's father. A lot of people came by the house to "party" with the father, and Gary found it hard to say no and not join in. When he couldn't keep up with his school assignments, he felt hopeless and doomed to repeat the same pattern he had experienced many times before.

I could have worked directly with Gary's moods — his feelings of depression and hopelessness — but I saw Gary's problem as being relational. Growing up in an unpredictable and emotionally unsupportive family environment left Gary primed for disorganization and chaos rather than for discipline and healthy boundaries. He needed a new story about how he could find support and structure through a relationship. And so I came up with a homework assignment for him: he was to find someone at the campus willing to help him put together a study schedule. Gary was hesitant at first because he felt out of place at the school, and he worried he might be judged negatively for not knowing how to create a study schedule. But Gary prided himself on being street smart, and so I asked him to draw upon his street smarts to find a resource — whether at the student guidance center or elsewhere.

During our next session, the first thing Gary did was to open a binder and display a weekly calendar showing his classes and study times. "I went to the student rec center," he told me, beaming. "I asked around to see if anyone knew how to put together a study schedule. Someone volunteered, and this is what we came up with." This laid the foundation for the next step — learning how to set boundaries and minimize the chaos where he was living. Later, I had Gary put into words the story of how he cultivated a positive relationship and willingly accepted help from others. Gary found a host of new strengths in this story — honesty with others, openness, motivation, effort, effectiveness, organization, trust, and the ability to find resources, to name a few. He started recognizing and appreciating his ordinary and life-sustaining daily strengths. Personally, I felt honored to work with Gary. He had learned to apply his strengths in order to shape a new, positive life story.

As Gary's story illustrates, strengths plant new seeds in our mental garden while simultaneously pulling out old, limiting stories by the roots. I should add, recognizing your strengths is not the same as bragging. The reason for locating your strengths is not to give yourself a phony ego boost so you can feel superior or compare yourself favorably to others. That would simply serve as a temporary and unsatisfying way to get the elevator to go up. Rather, you notice your strengths in order to get a more accurate representation and understanding of the things you *really* do during your day. Oddly, many people diminish their actual strengths, either ignoring them or simply saying, "Well, that's just my routine. I do that every day, so it's not really a strength."

While personal character strengths take a backseat in our often-hectic, self-critical, and achievement-oriented culture, they are akin to the nutrient-rich soil that is required for growing healthy plants. Your strengths are not measured by the Herculean tasks you accomplish. They are the small, daily tools you use to navigate with courage and perseverance through each ordinary day. They are a testament to the skills that help you fight through emotional clutter in order to be effective, confident, and productive. Here are a few examples:

- Inviting a friend for coffee (strength of hospitality)
- Taking the dog for a walk (strength of caring)
- Remembering where the car is parked at the mall (strength of memory)
- Making the bed in the morning (strengths of orderliness and cleanliness)
- Creating a grocery list (strength of planning)
- Knowing how to ask for help (strength of finding resources)
- Showing up for work (strength of discipline)
- Finishing a homework assignment or a work project (strengths of focus and concentration)
- Telling someone you appreciate them (strengths of love and gratitude)

The Lifestyle Tool that follows will help you discover how to transform any story into a story of strengths. And you'll be able to identify the strengths of others — a wonderful relationship-building practice.

LIFESTYLE TOOL: Growing Your Strengths Garden with Stories

Stories can prime us for feeling either safe or scared, trusting or defensive, open or closed. Stories that shine the light on our own strengths — and those of others — help us to have a better sense of confidence, self-esteem, and efficacy. What is more, this Lifestyle Tool gives us a new lens through which to understand and appreciate the strengths of others. This is a potent skill for sweeping away old stories filled with emotional clutter and replacing them with accurate stories that reflect your real-world abilities.

To start cultivating your strengths garden, think about a recent appointment that you went to. It doesn't matter what the appointment was for; any will suffice — whether it was meeting a friend for coffee, attending a business meeting, going to work in the morning, or showing up to vote for an election. When working with clients, I have them share the story of coming to the therapy session; when working with professionals, I have them share the story of coming to the workshop training.

Part 1

You may believe that going to an appointment is mundane and ordinary, even boring. By telling your story in the following way, you will discover that it says a lot about your strengths.

Write down, perhaps in a journal, the story of going to your appointment, and include the following six elements in your description:

1. What was your *personal history* around this appointment?

    For example, you may have had a history — that is, old emotional clutter — related to something you found unpleasant, such as getting up for an early-morning appointment, getting on the freeway, dealing with rush-hour traffic, parking, the weather, or concerns about who you were meeting. How did you manage to get to your appointment despite whatever was challenging? Did you prepare ahead or think about finding parking in advance? What strategies did you use?

2.   What *stressors* did you experience leading up to the appointment?

For instance, did you get enough sleep the night before your appointment? If this was a factor, did you make the effort to sleep? Did you get enough nutrition? Did you take care of your personal hygiene before the meeting? Did you wear clothing that helped you cope with the weather or just lifted your mood?

3.   What *thoughts* and *moods* did you experience before the appointment?

We never stand in the same river of thoughts or moods for very long, so how did you deal with any negative feelings or attitudes that popped up?

4.   What did your *body* feel like on the day of the appointment?

Did you have aches or pains in the body? How did you meet this challenge and still get to your appointment?

5.   What *responsibilities* and *obligations* did you attend to in order to get to the appointment?

Did you care for or attend to someone in your household who needed your help before going to the appointment? Did you get up early to walk the dog or take care of any pets?

6.   What methods for *centering* or finding *calm* or *joy* did you use leading up to the appointment?

Did you listen to music that helped calm or center you while traveling to the appointment? Did you get up early so as to have a little "quiet" time or so you could exercise or attend to personal self-care? Did you engage in any kind of centering ritual — such as having a warm cup of coffee or tea — that helped you on the day of your appointment?

Part 2

Now go back over what you have written, and identify the different strengths that you exhibited during the day that helped you get to your appointment. This is not a time for humility. You are assessing strengths, so see how many different strengths you can notice. The more, the better. After listing all your strengths, ask yourself these questions:

- How do I feel after noticing my strengths?
- How often have I taken any of these for granted in the past?
- What was the most surprising strength that I noticed?
- If someone other than myself had these strengths, what would I think of him or her?
- What new story does this tell about me?
- How can I begin to notice my strengths on a daily basis?

Part 3

As a daily lifestyle skill, give yourself what I like to call "The Strengths Challenge." As you go through your day, keep note of your strengths. Write them on a sheet of paper, or note them on your cell phone. See how many different strengths you can name, keep a record of them, and then review and appreciate them at the end of the week.

Separately, see if you can notice a single strength possessed by everyone you meet today, and don't keep it to yourself. Share that strength in your conversation with others. Notice how it makes them feel — and how it makes you feel. By complimenting others in this way, you are building relationships while exhibiting the strengths of *listening attentively to others* and *generosity of spirit*. How wonderful!

∞

Chapter 4

THE PEACE OF ACCEPTANCE

We can rent our grievances the master bedroom and build them a hot tub out back. We can give them a great lease with terrific terms that never expire, or we can grant them only a day-to-day tenancy.

— Fred Luskin, *Forgive for Good*

C an you picture a cartoon character like Bugs Bunny in a psychotherapy session? I imagine the conversation might go like this:

"Eh, so tell me…," Bugs says. "What's up with me, Doc?"

"Well, my long-eared friend, I've finally found what troubles you."

"Yeah?" Bugs says, munching on a carrot. "And what's that, Doc?"

"You live in a world of complete make-believe."

"Hey, Doc, that's great. And by the way, don't bother sending me the bill because this never happened!"

Nonacceptance is much like living in an illusory, "what if" world of make-believe. Much of the clutter of discomfort, discontent, and conflict that we experience in life comes from our unwillingness to accept things as they are. We ignore, push away, or reject that part of our experience we don't like. However, we can also choose to live in the "what is." We can stop fighting and resisting what is before us. Being present with "what is" gives a glimpse of the wholeness of our human experience, however messy it may be, and lets us fully touch this moment. This requires engaging three key mindfulness skills from PAIR UP, namely Attuned Acceptance, Reflection, and Understanding of Suffering. Together, these will change your relationship to unwanted emotional clutter.

At its core, the practice of acceptance is grounded in self-knowledge and self-observation. With acceptance, we see the truth about our mental clutter and our attachments to what we think is good and bad, beautiful and ugly, worthwhile and worthless. With acceptance, we roll down the windows of the car to smell the air, to get closer to what's happening instead of wrapping ourselves in a closed-off cocoon. We don't ignore what we find deplorable, sad, and unjust, but at the same time, we soften our reactivity and how we view even those unwanted things.

In *Think on These Things*, world teacher and author Krishnamurti wrote:

> It is discovery to suddenly see yourself as you actually are: greedy, quarrelsome, angry, envious, stupid. To see the fact without trying to alter it, just to see exactly what you are is an astonishing revelation. From there you can go deeper and deeper, infinitely, because there is no end to self-knowledge.

Opening the window to acceptance can be scary. This is an exploration and Lifestyle Tool that can profoundly transform your life and clear out old clutter.

✦

It was a very busy day at the clinic, and I was seeing clients on the hour. Answering a call between sessions, I learned that my next morning appointment had canceled. Since I was not feeling as present with patients as I wanted to be, I decided that a walking meditation would help me get focused. So I walked down four blocks to the Willamette River. It was a bright, windswept day. The dark blue water moved briskly as I walked in a grassy field. But it was colder than I had anticipated, and I hadn't brought a jacket. As the chill air brushed against my face, my reactive mind quickly jumped in by stating, "It's really cold out. This isn't very pleasant."

Continuing my walk, there was another intrusion to my "perfect walking meditation." Near the grassy field was a playground where a handful of children were rollicking and enjoying themselves. However, my mind interpreted their shouts of joy as an annoyance, and I thought, "Those kids are really noisy. I wish they would be quiet. They're ruining my perfect walking meditation."

In that moment, the inner voice of nonacceptance had its golden opportunity. It jumped in and whispered a very subtle command: "Go back to the office. It's warmer and quieter there. You'll have a better meditation." I often refer to these very quick and automatic thoughts as "mind whispers" that can make us act as robots if we're not careful.

In that moment, just like a robot following a command, I started to turn back up the hill to my office. That is, until I became fully aware of the mind whisper and suddenly realized that I was pushing away my experience. I thought humorously, "Oh, this moment isn't good enough? Reality is not conforming to the way I would like it to be, and so I have to reject it for something better?" I actually laughed as I stood in the grassy field.

Right then, I continued my walking meditation, but with one major difference — I accepted all of my experience and let go of my need to control it. Instead of pushing away the cold air, I let it in; I felt it and was present with it. Rather than escaping the shrieks of the children, I let those in, too, softening to them as I would to falling raindrops. By being present with and accepting what was right before me, I enjoyed a wonderfully nourishing and centering walking meditation.

✦

I've found that the more I notice my thoughts, the more I catch those sly mind whispers that try to commandeer my actions and steal away each precious moment. Think for a moment about an experience you have pushed away or rejected. Maybe you met a friend for a meal and found yourself looking across the table at her entrée, thinking, "I wish I had ordered what she's having instead of my entrée." This is actually an apt metaphor for how easily we can push away the meal that life prepares for us.

What is it that you wish wasn't part of your life? What do you turn away from, or reject, because it doesn't fit with the way you would prefer things to be? Do you have a list of complaints and grievances directed toward yourself or others? Is there a rant of shortcomings and inadequacies that blares in your head when you look in the mirror or watch the evening news? Believe it or not, reactive, abusive, and self-blaming thoughts may be harming you and others more than you think.

While there has been a lot of research on the harm caused by sexual and physical abuse, the dangers of verbal abuse were not fully understood until recently. A study published in the *American Journal of Psychiatry* looked at over eight hundred young adults who had no history of sexual or physical abuse. Those subjects who had experienced verbal abuse from their peers — from middle school and high school — were found to suffer from a significant increase in symptoms of depression, anxiety, dissociation, hostility, anger, and even drug use. Researchers also found abnormalities in the brain's corpus callosum, the part of the brain that links the right and left hemispheres and is implicated in helping us interpret and process our feelings and emotions. In addition, the study compared the damaging effects of peer verbal abuse with studies of parental verbal abuse and found them to be basically equivalent. If the unkind words of others can have such a powerful effect, why would we suppose our inner world of self-directed thoughts would be any less potent?

THE HEALING SALVE OF SELF-ACCEPTANCE

As challenging as it may be to accept the external conditions of our life, clearing out rejecting inner self-talk requires real scrubbing power. This leads to another question to ask yourself: Where does the voice that compares ourselves to others — frequently in an unfair light — originally come from? You may believe these thoughts are your own, but they may not be.

When Jorge, a man in his early fifties, came to see me, the last thing he expected to discover was the origin of his self-critical thoughts. Jorge was dealing with depression in the aftermath of the failure of his small business. Early on, he shared with me a litany of reasons why he would fail to find another job. "I don't know how to do a job interview," he told me convincingly. "Compared to the young people I'm competing with for jobs, I'm barely computer literate. Anyone who learns that my business failed would see me as a loser. And the truth is, I'm not much of a businessman or I would still be in business. And don't forget the economy," he said, his voice growing loud like an exclamation point. "It stinks."

Jorge was surprised when I told him how impressed I was

with his list of reasons for not being able to get a job. I asked if he was willing to create his own "Top Ten" list of reasons why he couldn't move forward. Jorge was excited to create his own list. At our next session, I asked Jorge about his list. He took a yellow sheet of paper out of his pocket and unfolded it. As he peered at the list, Jorge looked up at me, shaking his head. "You know, I can't believe what happened when I looked at my list," he said.

"What do you mean? What happened?" I asked.

"Well, I realized that this is just the way my mother thinks!"

"Help me understand that," I answered.

"It's the negativity, thinking I'm not good enough, that the cards are stacked against me, and that I can never really succeed in life. She's saying those same exact things all the time. When I saw my list, I couldn't believe it. One thing is for sure — I don't want to think this way anymore!"

By getting some space from his thoughts and writing them down, Jorge was able to notice his thoughts in a dramatically new way. By reflecting inwardly, he realized that he had learned a style of thinking from his family and adopted their view of the world. Jorge's experience also sheds light on the persuasive power of thoughts: *If you tell yourself something long enough, you might end up believing it, even if it has no basis in truth.*

What does it mean to have self-acceptance? It doesn't mean accepting weakness, putting up with what we find unacceptable, or lowering our personal standards. That's exactly what our critical inner voice would say! Acceptance does not mean that you give up and do not try to improve yourself. It means being honest about your starting point as you gain more skills to change your life (and yourself) for the better, according to your standards or what you are striving to achieve. The critical inner voice inhibits the ability to grow and change because it does not accurately register what is factual or true.

Self-acceptance changes the rules of the game by ending the ego's constant war over what is good and bad in us, what is beautiful and ugly in us, and what is okay to let in and what is not. Acceptance doesn't seek to define us by a particular behavior. With self-acceptance, we invite in our whole self, both the unlikable and the lovable parts. We take a more gentle and diplomatic stance toward ourself, our goals, our limitations, our vulnerabilities, and so on.

Self-acceptance shines light on where we are too constricted, tight, and opinionated. It helps us transcend our problems by asking, "Where did this knot first get tied?" Most importantly, it gently guides us to detach from the problem as we accept it by letting it be and letting it go. Self-acceptance grows self-awareness, insight, and compassion. It doesn't condemn us because we may have adopted a certain style of thinking from our parents, or because we're not as good a singer, dancer, manager, engineer, or spouse as someone else.

The deeper lesson of self-acceptance is that everything is mixed, even us. Have you ever met anyone who was all good or all bad? We might want to make our heroes saintly, as if Mother Teresa, Buddha, and Martin Luther King had no flaws. But if we stand in the light, we also cast a shadow. Acceptance helps us to be less self-blaming and kinder toward even our less-enlightened thoughts and deeds. And as we awaken to our own ignorance, frailty, and reasons for suffering, how can we not also understand and accept the brokenness of others? Not to condone, but to accept.

GETTING REAL WITH AUTHENTIC ACCEPTANCE

A concept that harkens back to ancient Buddhism is that of the Eight Worldly Winds that blow throughout our lives. However much we may try, we can't avoid these winds, which consist of praise and blame, fame and disrepute, gain and loss, and pleasure and pain. Trying to only experience or hold on to the positive attributes of praise, fame, gain, and pleasure is fruitless. Likewise, attempting to avoid the discomfort that comes from blame, disrepute, loss, and pain is a waste of time and energy. Life serves a full menu, so we taste both sweet desserts and bitter dishes. As the gaming houses in Las Vegas know, the tables (and the odds) eventually turn.

As a presenter who speaks to the public and provides keynotes and trainings for professionals, I've experienced the perils of the worldly winds. When a talk goes smoothly and is well received by the audience, a voice of praise often tells me, "You're a wonderful speaker. They loved you. It's only a matter of time before Oprah calls." If a talk feels disconnected and the audience doesn't respond, a voice of blame may admonish me, "You were really boring today. They nearly fell asleep and didn't like you. Your speaking career is toast."

Becoming attached to either outcome leads to trouble. These experiences have helped me to practice authentic acceptance, which is to rest in the truth of what happens in each moment without trying to push it away or cling to it. That means accepting that audiences will have a variety of responses, some positive and some not. That means accepting that my own skill as a speaker is evolving, and whether or not I've done well, I'm always trying to improve. At a certain talk, I may not be happy that I wasn't quicker or better at responding to questions from the audience, but I can accept it. That's reality. That's being human. By being more real, I do my best not to get deluded by the ego clutter that blocks me from experiencing all that life offers up. This is the place from which our wisdom can take root, as well as the ground of being at peace with the way things are — even as we may work to change them. This is how we loosen the deep-rooted tendencies that keep us stuck in mental clutter.

LIFESTYLE TOOL: Meditation for Resting in Self-Acceptance

Right now, use this visualization to help find a place of peace with whatever inner or external grievance or experience you're rejecting — no matter how hurtful or traumatic. This meditation will help you be more present and accepting of the whole you.

Part 1

What is one thing that you cannot accept?

On a sheet of paper, write down what you cannot accept, or simply hold the thought in your mind. Be as specific as possible. Keep in mind that this can be a physical sensation, a situation, or an emotion. Here are a few examples:

- I am getting older and don't feel attractive.
- I'm not lovable, and I fear being alone.
- I worry about my marriage because my husband/wife is distant and cold.
- I hate that I didn't get promoted and my career isn't moving forward.
- I was harmed by _____, and I can't forgive or accept it.

Part 2

Follow the meditation below to access a greater sense of peace, a softer perspective, or even a more accurate understanding of your statement.

- Find a quiet place to sit.
- Slow your breathing. Picture yourself resting in a beautiful place of supreme, sublime, and spacious peacefulness. There is nothing in this place that can harm you. You are totally safe and protected here. This can be a real place that you love and where you feel safe, or it can be an imaginary place that you picture in your mind's eye.
- Now think about people who have helped you in your life. These are people who hold a deep wish for your well-being, health, and safety. Imagine that these individuals are near you, and it feels good to be near them. They can be family, friends, or neighbors from your past or present. You can even think about a spiritual individual that you admire, such as Gandhi, Martin Luther King, or Jesus. They, too, if they could be here, would send you the warmest wishes for your well-being and safety.
- Let in the blessings and wishes for your well-being from this group that cares about you. Let this in as a feeling of warmth that seeps down into your cells. Breathe in the wishes for your well-being, letting them fill up the heart center with a warm glow. Let this warm glow of being loved and cared for spread throughout your body.
- Now notice that thing you cannot accept as being far, far off in the distance. It appears small and insignificant from such a distance.
- Next, imagine that the glow of warmth, love, and blessings around you expands, almost like a bubble. The bubble's golden glow feels warm and inviting. This is your bubble of self-acceptance, wisdom, and understanding that can safely encompass anything, no matter how difficult or unwanted.

- Imagine the bubble of self-acceptance growing and expanding around you. All your thoughts, your past, your emotions — positive or negative — are surrounded by the bubble, letting you just be with them all. Feel a sense of expansion and peace as the bubble grows.
- Watch as the bubble of self-acceptance takes in more and more. Once anything is inside the bubble, you no longer have to react to it, but you can freely notice it with kindness, greater understanding, and compassion.
- Let the bubble expand farther and farther, until it reaches all the way out to the difficult thing that you cannot accept. Feel what it's like as the bubble makes contact and softens in order to allow this thing inside. Imagine the bubble is accepting in the same way that a loving parent, best friend, compassionate mentor, or spiritual teacher accepts you for who you are.
- Let yourself come to peace and rest with all that is inside the bubble. Now, let the bubble expand and grow even beyond the horizon of the beautiful and serene place of peace where you sit. Now, everything is within the bubble, and there is no inside or outside, no pushing or pulling, no good or bad you, no winning or losing, in this all-inclusive, self-accepting, and loving place.
- Continue to breathe slowly for as long as you would like. Set the intention to accept your difficult situation as a *starting point*, not an end point. Let your own wisdom guide you as to how to move forward. When you are ready to conclude this visualization, give thanks to your bubble of self-acceptance, knowing you can return to it and rest in its spaciousness and warmth anytime you wish.

∞

Chapter 5

GET CENTERED
IN YOUR BREATH AND BODY

You see, consciousness thinks it's running the shop. But it's a second-ary organ of a total human being, and it must not put itself in control. It must submit and serve the humanity of the body. When it does put itself in control, you get a man like Darth Vader in *Star Wars*.
— Joseph Campbell, *The Power of Myth*

Did you count the number of thoughts you had this morning? You may laugh at this question because you've likely been inundated with thoughts since the moment you woke up. The brain is fast. So fast, in fact, that it has been estimated we can have as many as 25 to 125 thoughts *per second*. The Buddha thought we could have up to 3,000 thoughts per second. When I mentioned that in a workshop, a woman raised her hand and said, "I have four thousand." We all laughed, but it sure seems that way, and it brings a whole new dimension to the concept of mental clutter.

If each of us had a penny for our every thought, we'd all be wealthy. Instead, we are often worn down by our thoughts, frayed by anxious ones, and fretting from persistent ones that clutch onto us like frightened children. Fortunately, we have an innate, built-in way to rest the weary mind. It's achieved when we drop into — or get grounded in — the body. The body cooperates with the brain if we let it. Like a copilot, it can alert us to when we are out of balance and about to encounter turbulence — and it can guide us toward a smoother flight path and a place of harmony.

One patient I worked with, Emily, learned to use her body as a copilot. Emily was a devoted, young mother of a six-year-old daughter, and if I had to choose a movie to describe how Emily's mind worked when I first met her, it would be *Runaway Train*. Emily was so consumed with fear over her daughter's safety and health that her mind was always spinning out of control and ready to go off the rails. This produced constant and debilitating panic attacks. Emily certainly wasn't alone in her suffering. Anxiety is the number-one mental health issue in the United States, with some 40 million persons suffering from some kind of anxiety disorder. If Emily's daughter went to a friend's home for a sleepover, Emily would be besieged by thoughts of potential harm. These thoughts were often creative, if not bizarre, such as imagining her daughter falling out of the window at her friend's house and having her eye punctured by a shard of glass that was hidden in the grass. If her child rode the bus to school, she imagined a gory traffic accident.

I worked with Emily using several modalities. To begin, she practiced Inner-Facebooking so she could learn to notice her thoughts from a distance and judge their accuracy. But what really made a difference was when she dropped into the body. She connected with her body through her breath, which she used to turn on the body's relaxation response — the parasympathetic nervous system — so she could switch off panic attacks on command as well as prevent them from occurring. She discovered how to make the body her friend and trusted copilot.

It all came together for her one day when she took her daughter to the community center. "I was driving my girl to soccer practice," she explained to me, "when I felt this very slight sensation of tightness in my chest. I also noticed how tightly I was gripping the steering wheel. Suddenly, it came to me what I was thinking about. I was thinking about a horrible accident happening at the soccer field. So I relaxed my hands and body and started the belly breathing. Before, I never would have noticed those things. I was working my way up to a panic attack without even knowing it." This was a major turning point for Emily. By listening to her copilot (her body), she became aware that she was running into rough weather — old mental clutter that was preprogrammed to create an anxious story.

Using enhanced body awareness is like setting a brand-new preset on your TV or adding a new "favorites" bookmark on your web browser. It tunes you in to the present moment instead of what neuroscientists call "the default mode network" — a state of mind wandering that spins stories. This default mode usually occurs when you're not focused on a specific mental task — like writing up a report, doing homework, or planning a trip. The default mode, however, is not always random. If you have a preset station you frequently visit, such as the Anxiety Channel or the Depression Network, then it's easy to tune in to your default preset and not even know it.

BREATH: THE PRESENT-MOMENT CHANNEL

Suppose your doctor told you about a new miracle medication proven to reduce negative thinking and depression as well as potentially lengthen your life span — and it had absolutely no negative side effects. Would you take it? That's just what we're learning about the healing capabilities of breathing and present-moment awareness. A study in *Cognitive Therapy and Research Journal* found that the practice of mindful breathing — being present with the breath while breathing diaphragmatically — actually decreased rumination, repetitive negative thoughts, and depression. It even reduced fear around sensations in the body.

Meanwhile, a study published in *Clinical Psychological Science* showed how present-moment awareness just might act as a fountain of youth that keeps us biologically younger despite our chronological age. Researchers at the University of California, San Francisco (UCSF), looked at the effects of mind wandering on the telomeres of over two hundred healthy women. What are telomeres? They are tiny DNA-based tips found at the ends of our chromosomes. They hold the cell together, much like that plastic tip at the end of a shoelace. Telomeres are a biological measure of aging, and when they shorten or fray, the cell no longer properly divides, causing sickness and death.

Previous studies have demonstrated that severe stress prematurely shortens telomeres and accelerates aging in blood cells by up to ten years. The study at UCSF found that mind wandering also prematurely shortened telomeres. But there's good news. They found that being focused, engaged, and present in the moment protects our telomeres and keeps them from dwindling. Researchers concluded, "Those who reported high mind wandering had shorter telomeres, consistently across immune cell types (granulocytes, lymphocytes), than did those who reported low mind wandering, even after adjusting for stress....A present attentional state may promote a healthy biochemical milieu and, in turn, cell longevity."

Now, before you get all stressed-out over how frequently your mind wanders, let me qualify that *negative mind wandering* — worry about the past and anxiety about the future — is what has a harmful effect on aging. Sustaining present-moment focus is good for you, whether it's engaging in a pleasant daydream, a creative thought, planning for your vacation, or taking this next breath.

In addition, it may be possible for telomeres to lengthen. One preliminary study showed that a lifestyle intervention that included stress reduction and breathing practices, exercise, social support, and healthy eating actually lengthened telomeres. There is more coming in this area of research, but the key message is that our daily experiences and how we use our awareness profoundly affects us at the cellular level.

Have you ever watched a baby breathe? If you watch closely, you'll see that the belly moves in and out, not the chest. This means the baby is taking a nice, long, slow breath; without any training, babies breath diaphragmatically. This is our natural, default breathing method, and when you breathe this way, you automatically reduce mind wandering as well as turn on the body's relaxation system — the parasympathetic nervous system. Who says that newborns aren't smart?

But over time, by encountering stress, our breath gets shallow and goes into the upper part of the lungs. If you picture your lungs like a cup, then taking a shallow breath is filling up only the top of the cup. Shallow breathing makes us vulnerable to the sympathetic nervous system and activates the body's stress response. When this happens, our blood pressure, pulse rate, and respiration rate increase. Our body and brain then get hyped up on stress hormones, even during an average day. The secret to belly breathing is to fill up that cup from the bottom, just like we did when we were young.

Now let's explore getting present with the breath. This is an essential Lifestyle Tool that is both portable and powerful.

LIFESTYLE TOOL: Breathing for Presence and Peace

Fortunately, it's easy to relearn belly breathing by experimenting with changes in body posture. Here are four alternate postures that will help you rediscover your youthful breathing technique. Each of the methods below will help you pull back your shoulders and stretch some muscles between the rib cage (the intercostals) that hinge the rib cage open. This makes it easier to do belly breathing. This method of breathing is also called diaphragmatic breathing.

After you practice and learn how to breathe in this way, you can make this your new default, preset breathing method. This will prepare you for handling life's difficulties with greater clarity, calm, and awareness.

Posture 1

Standing or sitting, place your arms behind your back and clasp your hands together. Don't force the breath. See if your breath slows down and if there's movement in the abdominal area. If you have learned to "suck it in," give yourself permission to relax the abdominal muscles, and let your belly be free. If you have been breathing shallowly for years, it might take some time for you to consistently get that slow, long breath. (Note: If you're having trouble getting the breath into the lower part of the belly while using the postures included here, try lying on your back or side, which makes it easier to feel the belly move in and out. Once you've got the belly moving, try these postures again.)

Posture 2

I call this the Wonder Woman or superhero posture. Place your hands at the sides of your ribs. Finding the lowest rib, position both hands at that lowest rib with your elbows facing outward.

As you breathe, do you notice the sides of the abdomen moving outward? This longer breath gives you ten times more air than if you were to breathe shallowly. This posture is nice for those who don't want to focus on the belly moving outward.

Posture 3

Raise your arms up and cradle your hands behind your head or neck. Alternately, you can keep the arms raised and touch your shoulders with your fingertips. For some, this is an effective way of getting that deeper breath. If for any reason you feel light-headed or dizzy, you may be taking *too* deep a breath. Imagine your lungs are a cup. You are filling the cup from the bottom slowly, but not all the way to the brim.

Posture 4

I call this last method "bellows breathing" because you use your arms like an accordion or bellows that opens wide as you inhale and closes as you exhale. The Navy SEAL who demonstrated this for me said that the SEALs use breathing as a means of "arousal control" so they can continue to think clearly even when experiencing fear and anxiety during a mission. Here's how it works. Start by placing your palms together in front of your chest. Open the accordion by moving your arms out to your sides as you take a nice, full belly breath. Keep your arms at your sides as you hold your breath for the count of two. Then close the accordion by slowly bringing your arms together as you exhale on the count of four — as your hands return to their position in front of your chest. Practice taking two or three of the accordion breaths.

Use these four different techniques throughout the day. Above all, have patience. It can take time to retrain your body to breathe in these ways.

I also suggest scheduling breathing breaks throughout the day. As I ask people in my workshops: You spend time taking care of your physical hygiene by brushing your teeth and taking a shower. Isn't it worth three minutes a day to take care of your mental hygiene?

Breathing is mental flossing. Schedule three minutes of belly breathing a day. You can do one minute in the morning, one minute in the afternoon, and one minute in the evening. It's that easy to start. Then, during your day, notice where your breath is, then bring it down to the belly. You'll be getting into your body, getting more present, and scrubbing out mental clutter with this all-purpose cleaner. You'll also be following the advice of Henry David Thoreau, who in 1859 wrote in his journal, "You must live in the present, launch yourself on every wave, find your eternity in each moment."

∞

—— *Part 2* ——

HEALING RELATIONAL, CULTURAL, AND ANCESTRAL CLUTTER

We are much more than the product of our personal biological, physical, and psychological processes. In truth, we exist in a milieu, an intricate web of life. We may never fully understand the extent to which the past influences our experiences and choices, but we can begin by honoring and empathizing with those who preceded us. By bringing awareness to ancient clutter, we take the first step toward healing, hopefulness, and evolving a new way of being — which we can then pass on to those following in our footsteps and our heartbeats.

Chapter 6

CLEANSING FAMILY EMOTIONAL CLUTTER

To survive the time in the woods, your old ways must die. Initiation...
is an inner pilgrimage where you free yourself from that which ties you
to habitual and even harmful ways of being.
— Julie Tallard Johnson, *Wheel of Initiation*

The intimate connection we have with family gets embedded within our very being long before we can utter a word. Much of this initial wiring occurs in the right hemisphere of our brain in the first ten to twenty-four months of life. That's when our brain begins to develop an emotional and social program, or template, as it syncs up, or attunes, with our mother, father, and other caregivers.

It's no wonder that trying to untangle and separate ourselves from family can leave us humbled. Attempting to clear out family emotional clutter can feel like going for a hike in the woods without a compass: frightening, scary, and disorienting. As limiting, harmful, irritating, and downright confounding as family clutter can be, there's still something oddly comfortable about it. It is, after all, a representation of our earliest experiences of home and attachment to others.

For this reason, your journey into clearing family clutter can be understood as a powerful initiation. By gaining deeper awareness, compassion, and insight into your family, you can shift into how you will manifest your future. Let's begin the journey by exploring how the young brain receives its initial programming for how to manage emotions and relationships.

Essentially, if our caregivers are responsive, caring, available, and attentive and provide a secure environment, then our brain mirrors that. The program that gets downloaded into our brain's hard drive says, "I feel confident and convinced that I can get my needs met. I feel secure because others respond reliably, predictably, cooperatively, and generously. The world is a safe place where I can trust others, and I can feel protected and believe that I can thrive in the presence of others."

But suppose our caregivers are confused, frustrated, anxious, neglectful, or emotionally unavailable. In this scenario, our right hemisphere sets up its initial download very differently. The resulting social and emotional program says, "Getting my needs met is frustrating, scary, and confusing. I feel insecure because others react unpredictably, hurtfully, erratically, and selfishly. The world is a dangerous and strange place where I can't trust others, and I better be on high alert in order to survive."

Our caregiver's ability or inability to relate is mirrored in our own mind. As a result, we may grow up feeling either mostly secure or insecure in relationships. But this brain program may have sources that go far beyond our immediate parents or caregivers. And this holds the key to letting go of family emotional clutter.

EPIGENETICS: A NEW CONTEXT
FOR FORGIVENESS AND CHANGE

It can be disheartening to witness the repetition of cruelty and brutality that erupts and reenacts in society during our lifetime. We often attribute this to bad dictators, lack of democracy, survival of the fittest, or socioeconomic reasons. Some propose that humans are just violent by nature and it's in our genes. The new science of epigenetics paints a radically different picture. It suggests that our very *behavior* and *environment* can alter our genes. This means that impulses like violence, for example, are not necessarily hardwired into human nature — but they may actually be predispositions that can be changed.

The word *epigenetics* translates as "over" or "above" the gene. Basically, our genome is like the hardware of a computer — the DNA. The epigenome acts as a software program that instructs our genes what to do, such as whether they should turn on or off. Research illustrates how our daily experiences — the foods we eat, how we breathe, how we respond to stress, and how we interact with the environment — deliver the instructions that tell our genes how to express themselves. In some cases, these new instructions will be passed along to the next generation — without requiring any genetic mutation. Epigenetics may hold the key to making the sage advice from Einstein a reality: "Peace cannot be kept by force; it can only be achieved by understanding."

Research at Duke University, conducted by scientist Randy Jirtle, examined how food acts as an epigenetic software program. Jirtle tested how diet affected a particular health-related gene — the agouti gene — in rats. Because the rat's coat color was also controlled by this same gene, Jirtle could visually distinguish if the agouti gene was actively turned on (and rats had a yellow coat) or shut off (and they had a brown coat). When the agouti gene is turned on, rats feature a distinctly yellow coat as well as suffer from obesity and a drastically shortened life span. To shut off the obesity-producing gene, yellow-coated rats were fed a diet rich in methyl groups (a molecule of one carbon and three hydrogen atoms). The methyl groups attached to the agouti gene and deactivated it. Here's the amazing thing: this methyl-rich diet also altered future generations by producing thinner and healthier rats. This next generation also had brown coats — a tracer telling the scientists that the agouti gene remained turned off and had been deactivated by diet. However, if the now-healthy, brown-coated rats were fed a poor diet, the agouti gene got turned on again — and this was also passed along to offspring, who sported yellow coats, obesity, and a shorter life span. Jirtle's work shows that nutritional and environmental factors can alter how our genes get expressed. And it proves that these factors are inheritable. There are even epigenetic medical interventions that turn off genes that cause some kinds of cancer.

Other research using animal models shows how being nurtured (or not being nurtured) can alter the development of critical areas in the brain — and that these epigenetic changes are then passed along to the next generation. In *The Science of the Art of Psychotherapy*, child development researcher Allan Schore writes, "We know that massive increases in stress hormones have a detrimental effect on brain development. This represents the psychobiological intergenerational transmission of a predisposition to violence and to depression." Keep in mind that a person's DNA is not mutating or changing. It's the expression of the gene that is changing due to interaction with the environment.

This is a powerful and hopeful message. But with greater hope comes greater personal responsibility with regard to our life choices. Thoughtless choices or toxic behaviors might not only affect our own health but the health of our children and grandchildren.

Still, the question remains: how do we live with the pain and suffering that exist in our family — even from those who may have no interest in acknowledging or changing their hurtful behaviors?

If we keep blaming others, healing will be difficult. But the epigenetic context paints a different picture. It asks: How is blame really helpful? How far back in our family history should we point an angry finger? A hundred years? A thousand? A better approach may be to compassionately recognize that when we look at faded photos of our relatives, we are really looking at ourselves. Our personal struggles are connected to the larger, universal web of our parents, grandparents, and all of humanity.

If we learn anything from epigenetics, it is that we are not fated to follow the genetic footsteps of ghosts past. With the power of aware choice, intention, and attuned attachment, we can alter our behavior, if not provide a more enlightened genetic expression — and enriched life — to those who follow.

AWARENESS AND CHANGE VERSUS FORGIVENESS

I've never had the greatest memory in the world — far from it. But there's one memorable conversation I won't soon forget. It was with my good friend Stephen, a former Marine and avid runner who projected the kind of confident physical presence you might expect. He was the father of three adult children whom I had met at his son's wedding. I could feel the respect and love that existed between Stephen and his children. This mutually nurturing relationship was possible despite a hidden history of abuse.

On one particular morning over a cup of coffee, Stephen and I started talking about father-son relationships when my friend grew silent. His face appeared ashen as his eyes looked upward as if going back in time. "My father sexually abused me when I was a boy," he said softly. Then he let out a sigh and said, "I vowed

I would never do that to my children or hurt them in any way."
When I asked if he was still bitter, he answered, "I released it, and
I got to a place of tolerance. Besides, shit happens."

Stephen hadn't forgiven his father, but he accepted what happened and learned to let it go. It was not in the foreground of
his thoughts. He came to peace with his messy family emotional
trauma in his own way. I gained even more respect for Stephen
that day. His story shows that having a messy and abusive family
history is neither an excuse for abusive behavior nor need it be a
predictor of the choices we will make.

✦

The ability to cultivate feelings of safety and trust with others is a
Lifestyle Tool that anyone can learn. This doesn't mean you need
to forgive those who have hurt you, but you owe it to yourself not
to let a history of emotional clutter keep you stuck in unhealthy
relationships. Before introducing this chapter's Lifestyle Tool, I
want to share the story of a client of mine who experienced abuse
in his marriage.

Tom was a fifty-eight-year-old professional whose wife constantly exploded with anger. She used her anger to control him by
throwing emotional tantrums and berating him in front of others.
He felt as if he were constantly walking on eggshells. As I learned
more about Tom's family history, it became clear that he was repeating an old family pattern. Tom's parents — Ed and Betty —
had actually modeled the codependent relationship that Tom was
enmeshed in. Whenever Tom's father, Ed, verbally abused Betty,
she always excused and quickly forgot his unacceptable behavior.
What's more, Betty's own father was an alcoholic who both physically and verbally abused Betty's mother.

Eventually, Tom began to notice how, just like his mother,
he developed a kind of abuse amnesia — either easily excusing

or forgetting about his spouse's inappropriate behavior. To help Tom overcome his amnesia, I encouraged him to chronicle events as they occurred, as well as the abusive events he tended to forget. Tom recovered from his "amnesia" by documenting the events and rereading them. This gave him a new perspective on what was happening.

One day, he brought several pages of "remembrance notes" with him into a session. "I can't believe I've allowed myself to be treated this way," he said, shaking his head. "This is not healthy or loving. It may be part of my family history, but now is the time to change it." It wasn't easy for Tom to advocate for himself, but when he did, his wife was unwilling to change. The marriage came to an end, and Tom was terribly saddened by the loss — because in his family, you stuck to a marriage no matter how bad things got. At the same time, Tom was excited to break through ancient family clutter. Most of all, he gained an understanding of how to create mutually happy and healthy relationships.

LIFESTYLE TOOL: Cleansing Family Clutter by Downloading an Updated Brain Program

Do not look for bad company
Or live with men who do not care.
Find friends who love the truth.

— Buddha, *The Dhammapada*

What if the early childhood social and emotional programming that got downloaded into your brain is not helping you? Are you simply out of luck? Fortunately, that initial program can be deleted and replaced with the newest relationship and emotional safety program. You just need to know the secret of where to find it and how to install the new download.

Part 1

You won't find the program on the shelf at your local computer store or on the internet. That's because it's a living, breathing program that exists *within* certain people who act as true benefactors to those around them. Who are these benefactors? How can you identify them? Here are a few qualities to look for:

- Benefactors are people who, when you are in their presence, make you feel good and also safe.
- Benefactors feel at ease in their own skin.
- Benefactors are individuals who smile frequently and truly listen when you talk.
- You feel a sense of mutuality with benefactors — it's not all about them, their life, and their issues.
- Benefactors demonstrate empathy — by understanding what others are feeling. They tend to act compassionately on behalf of others. Maybe they volunteer at a food bank or lend a hand when a friend is sick.
- Benefactors are open-minded and not rigidly stuck in their viewpoint or dogma. Benefactors don't exclude or harshly judge someone because of differences of religion, opinion, or political persuasion.
- Benefactors are often resilient and forgiving. The ups and downs of life, as well as the injustices that occur, don't leave permanent scars on their psyche. They have learned to accept and forgive.
- Finally, benefactors are supportive and happy for your successes — not jealous or envious. This means they may act as a resource or mentor in some area of your life.

This is not to say benefactors are saints and don't have blind spots. We all have blind spots. But a life outlook that is optimistic, curious, and enthusiastic often overshadows these limitations.

In addition, you don't need to find someone who ideally embodies every attribute above. What's important is identifying people who, by and large, are open and engaging with others and who are kind and make you feel safe in their presence.

Now, here's the challenging part. Evaluate the people closest to you in your life: Are they benefactors who help you access this new program? Or do they run the old program that says, "Others react unpredictably, hurtfully, erratically, and selfishly. The world is a dangerous and strange place where I can't trust others, and I better be on high alert to survive." Of course, these individuals may care about you deeply and be faithful and loyal friends, but if they are running this old program, they may be making it difficult for you to delete it in yourself.

For now, simply be aware of any people in your life who are running this old program. You don't necessarily need to do or change anything about your relationship with them, but you want to be aware that these people don't embody what you need right now. If someone is really, really holding you back, is obviously unsupportive, and is so negative and judgmental that you don't feel respected and safe, then you may need to make an immediate change. But this Lifestyle Tool is focused on fostering the supportive and resilient people who can help you download a new program. Further, as you successfully reprogram yourself, you can potentially become a benefactor for others, possibly helping those wounded survivors in your life. Being a wounded soul isn't a bad thing — a lot of our humanity comes from our woundedness.

Part 2

Once you've located a benefactor, you're halfway there. The next goal is to download the program they're running. You do that through attuning with them. Our brains have a wonderful ability to experience, or mirror, what others are feeling. This is a natural ability we all possess. To a degree, this means copying and emulating benefactors, but it does not mean giving up your own identity or free will. You remain your own separate, individual self, and you make your own decisions, but you allow yourself to attune to the sense of safety, trust, and compassion that this other person feels and embodies. This lets you experience this upgrade, and you can decide for yourself how it feels and what to do about it.

Follow the steps below to attune and get the upgraded program. When in the presence of these individuals, or benefactors, you will:

- Set the conscious intention to notice what the benefactor is feeling as you talk or interact with this person.
- Pay special attention to facial expressions and body language. It's okay if you experiment with similar body language to see how that makes you feel.
- Allow yourself to have a range of emotions and facial expressions as you interact.
- Allow yourself and your body to relax. Take some calming breaths. Notice if this other person has relaxed breathing. It can even help to mirror or match your breath to that of the benefactor.
- Look around your environment and remind yourself that you are safe. This will quiet your brain's smoke detector. Do this as often as needed. You might even notice something about the room that you find pleasant — such as a color, shape, or object.
- Pay attention to the stories that a benefactor shares. Notice if these stories include how others helped the person to reach his or her goals or overcome obstacles.
- When sharing a story of your own, make sure to mention the resources and people who helped you.
- As you listen to a benefactor's stories, imagine yourself

going through the same experience. With empathy, let
yourself notice how that helps you better understand the
other person. If this understanding gives you a fresh insight that you want to share, do so.

• When leaving, let this person know you enjoyed the
meeting. This gives a nice sense of closure and safety as
you prepare to leave.

By attuning, you create new neural connections, rewire the
brain, and install healthy emotions and feelings of safety within.
Be patient. You don't have to be perfect with this. Each time you
attune with a benefactor, you can get another program upgrade.
You can also practice by running the program when you are with
others. Above all, enjoy the process.

∞

Chapter 7

REFLECTIONS ON COMPASSIONATE COMMUNICATION

Compassion, in Tibetan terms, is a spontaneous feeling of connection with all living things. What you feel, I feel; what I feel, you feel. There's no difference between us.

— Yongey Mingyur Rinpoche, *The Joy of Living*

I remember where I was on the day of the tragic shooting at Sandy Hook Elementary School in Newtown, Connecticut, on December 14, 2012. That sad event will forever be etched in my memory because on that day I was facilitating a mindfulness workshop. It so happened that one of the workshop participants got the news and shared it with the group. We were all badly shocked and shaken by it, and I suggested we sit in quiet for a minute or two, silently sending blessings for those involved.

One of the early-morning exercises I'd planned for that workshop was based on a touching story written in 1885 by Russian novelist Leo Tolstoy called "Three Questions." The story's message is to focus on helping the person standing at your side in this moment because life is precious and unpredictable. Because of the Sandy Hook news, I considered skipping over this exercise. But mindfulness means being with the hard and most tender parts of life, too. I decided to go ahead. While I got all choked up telling Tolstoy's story (as we all did), never was the truth of its message more evident than on that day. With that as background, I'd like to share the "Three Questions" story as I have adapted it for my workshops.

THREE QUESTIONS

The story is about a king who had a strong interest in philosophy. (You might imagine that his kingdom was located off in the woods not too far from where you live — centuries before modern settlers arrived.) The king wanted to find the conclusive answers to three questions so he could make wiser decisions. The three questions were:

What's the best time to do each thing?

Who are the most important people that one should work with?

What is the most important task to do at all times?

Being a savvy king, he offered up a very generous reward to anyone who could best answer these questions. The king's subjects got all excited about the contest. Soon, he was inundated with mail. All the answers were practical, but the king noticed that each contained a bias. Take, for example, the question, Who are the most important people that one should work with? Doctors wrote in saying that doctors were the most important because they healed people. Musicians said musicians were the most important because they helped people dance and feel good. The king realized that there must be an answer that offered a more universal truth.

It so happened that the king knew of a wise old hermit who lived on a hilltop in the woods. The king decided to find the hermit in order to get the answers he sought. Since the king didn't want anyone to know he was looking for the hermit, he dressed in peasant clothing and trekked out early in the morning, taking with him a trusted guard and attendant. Together they'd hiked quite a distance when they came upon a dense wood with a narrow path leading up a hill. The king had a feeling this was where the hermit lived, so he told his attendant and guard to wait as he stepped onto the trail.

It was an arduous journey, and the dense wood was very dark and eerie. Finally, the king reached a small clearing where the sun was shining through. Sure enough, there was the frail, old hermit, digging in a garden. The king immediately took pity on the man. He took the man's shovel and told the old man to rest. Then, as the king continued digging, he asked the hermit the three questions. But the hermit didn't reply. He just sat there, mute and expressionless. Before long, the sun was setting behind the trees, casting long shadows across the clearing. The king realized that it would soon be dark, and he would need to get back to the village. So again he asked the hermit the three questions, and again he got no reply.

The king suspected that maybe the hermit didn't know the answers or just didn't want to help him, so he prepared to leave. But just then, a sound came from the edge of the woods. The king and the hermit whirled around to see a wounded stranger stumbling through the brush and the bramble. The man was bleeding and barely conscious, and he fell right at the feet of the king. The king didn't hesitate. He cleaned the stranger's wound and even used his own shirt to stop the blood flow and bandage it. The king realized the man's life hung in the balance, and so he decided to stay the night and watch over the injured man in order to save his life. He made a fire to keep the man warm and gave him water throughout the night. Eventually, the man's breathing became regular and he slept.

As dawn came, the sun filtered through the morning trees and the birds woke up, filling the air with their melodious chirping. The stranger woke up, too. He looked up at the king, weakly pointed at him, and said words that shocked the king. "I know who you are. You're the king," he said, adding, "and I followed you here from the village to assassinate you. I waited for you to come back down the hill, but when you didn't, your guard spotted me and he wounded me."

"But why? Why would you want to do such a thing?" said the king, taken aback.

The stranger explained he lived in the nearby kingdom, which years before had gone to war with the king's homeland. "My brother died in that war," explained the man. "And I lost my home. And so I vowed to take revenge on you. But now you've saved my life, and I see that I had you all wrong. If you'd have me, I'd like to be in your service and be your loyal subject."

The king was so touched by this turn of events that he immediately forgave the stranger. The king then ran down the hill to get his guard and attendant. They carried the man back to his kingdom, but not before the king promised to give the man a home. The king also had his best physicians tend to the man and make sure he returned to full health.

After the man was carried off, the king stood, still in shock at all that had transpired. The king sighed, then looked at the hermit. "Well, I didn't get any answers from you, but at least we saved that man's life." As he turned to leave, the hermit finally spoke up. "But king, you just got the answers to your questions!"

"I did?" said the king with a puzzled expression.

"Yes," nodded the hermit. "If you had ignored me yesterday and left, that man would have been waiting to harm you. That means that the time spent working in my garden was the most important. That you took pity on my age meant I was the most important person. And your most vital task was to assist me. Later in the afternoon, when the injured man fell at your feet, the most pressing action was to save him. Don't you see? Now is the only time that matters. No one has control over any moment except this one. None of us owns or purchases the future, which is why the person who matters most is whoever is at your side. Right here. Right now. Finally, what should you endeavor to do at all times? Do what you can to ensure the happiness of the one who is right before you. Who can say whether such an opportunity will ever appear in the future?"

✦

Let yourself sit with this story for a few moments. What are you feeling? What are you thinking? How could you apply Tolstoy's advice when facing the difficult people in your life — those who cause you a lot of emotional pain and clutter?

The Gift of Kind Words and Compassionate Presence

Previously, we explored how abusive words harm the brain. Research shows that warm, soothing, and calming words can produce the opposite effect — quieting down the brain's smoke detector and preparing the brain for feelings of greater safety, trust, and security. Psychologists studying the process call this security priming. The idea is that you can prime someone to feel or think in a certain way. The idea of priming has been part of our lexicon for years. Many motorcycles and older vehicles, for example, require priming of the engine with a few extra turns of the throttle or pumps on the accelerator pedal before turning the ignition switch. Once the engine is primed with gas, the spark plugs can do their job, starting the engine.

The security priming process works in much the same way. It prepares the mind to spark positive feelings after exposing people to priming words in a variety of ways — such as through reading, seeing, and hearing the words. Security priming has even been shown to work subliminally — though it's not quite as effective. Priming through words has many applications.

Security priming has been shown to be useful for individuals who have experienced some kinds of childhood trauma. Even mistrustful individuals who have a history of conflict — such as Palestinians and Israelis — can become less wary of one another when they are first exposed to security priming words having to do with openness and protection. In *Attachment in Adulthood*, researchers Mario Mikulincer and Phillip Shaver examine how words like *closeness*, *love*, *caring*, and others can help adults who get anxious, avoidant, or angry when trying to communicate their needs. As a result of being exposed to priming words, these individuals can feel more trusting, safe, and secure, particularly when facing a difficulty. A study published in the *Journal of Personality and Social Psychology* found that feeling more secure — by using priming techniques — increased compassion, caregiving behaviors, and altruistic behavior.

Did you feel primed after reading "Three Questions"? Maybe so, but we get primed all the time, for good or for bad, by the media we're exposed to — by advertisements, video games, violence, the news, sports, and so on. The point is that priming affects how we think, feel, and act. It is one of the ways that we learn. Knowing this, why not securely prime ourselves as well as those we care about with stories of love, caring, and generosity?

Just being present with another in a caring and attentive way could be considered a kind of security priming that helps others feel safe. While we may not have it within our power to make someone happy, we can offer our compassionate presence. The origin of the word *compassion* is "to be with suffering."

Do you know anyone who has *not* suffered? If you possess a human body and a human mind, then you surely have experienced loss, grief, and sadness in life. I'm not trying to be morose. That's just the way it is. But it's not the whole story. This knowing binds us together. It means that you and that person who is walking down the street are not all that different. It also can give us the courage to accept loss and to deeply appreciate this moment — especially with that person standing at our side.

Tolstoy's story reminds us of a true gift each of us possesses — and can give to others. And yet, how many of us purposefully choose to sit with others in a compassionate manner, where no words are required? It's all too easy to go into autopilot mode when we are with another person. In fact, psychologists have identified the tendency for us to make mental shortcuts. This can have some advantages, but it might also result in making a snap judgment about another person. On autopilot, we might miss out on the beauty or uniqueness of another. Autopilot may feel safe, but it's surface-safe.

When was the last time you sat with another person — and had no other agenda than offering compassion? In my workshops, after introducing Tolstoy's "Three Questions," I do the following exercise: Everyone gets a partner. Then for three minutes partners sit in silence facing each other. When I describe what we're going to do, I can see the initial worry. But I remind people that this is not staring but an opportunity to be with another human in a deeply relational, compassionate, and open way. How do participants typically respond to this exercise afterward? How do you think you would respond? I've seen the gamut, including partners who could barely suppress their laughter, people who avoided looking at their partner's gaze, and others who said it was a profoundly transcendent experience akin to looking in a mirror.

Try this yourself, if you wish. If you do, make sure your partner understands the exercise and is honestly open to it. It's better to have no expectations; whether you and your partner discuss the experience afterward is up to you. However, it's enough to just reflect on Tolstoy's story, perhaps sharing your insights with the next person you meet or interact with. See if it changes how you express yourself, and appreciate that person who is at your side, right now.

LIFESTYLE TOOL: Priming Respectful and Kind Communication

Words are the tools by which we strengthen our relationships and prime others for feelings of safety. Wise speech primes us and others for trust; speech that is thoughtless and unkind produces pain and separation from others. Words that come from being impatient, angry, reactive, and demanding can push others away. If you have been on the receiving end of this (and who hasn't?), then you know how hurtful and harmful this can be to your relationships.

Below are five key aspects of engaging kind and wise speech:

1. **Speak at the right time.** More often than not, this can mean *not* speaking, especially during those times when you are feeling upset or reactive. It may be wiser for you to cool down by taking a short break. Come back when you are able to speak from a calmer perspective, when you can express yourself without escalating an argument or difference of opinion.

2. **Speak with honesty.** Honesty is the cornerstone of authentic and wise speech because it develops trust. This also means looking within and letting go of those obstacles to honesty, such as envy, greed, and self-interest. On the other hand, this does not mean justifying or saying

something hurtful by claiming you are only being "honest." That would simply be unkind or mean-spirited.

3. **Speak with kindness and affection.** Regardless of what you say, you can strive to express it with kindness and a gentle tone. It is important to express your feelings, but if you cannot speak calmly, then wait until you can use loving and gentle speech.

4. **Speak in a beneficial way.** Be careful and thoughtful about what you say. Make sure that your speech is beneficial, supportive, and compassionate. This means that it's important not to gossip or use words as a weapon.

5. **Speak with intention and from the heart.** Make a point of speaking in a respectful, nonblaming, and nonjudgmental way, even if you disagree with the other person. This lets all parties be heard and feel understood. This doesn't mean you can't defend yourself against verbal abuse, but foster and deepen friendship whenever possible.

To conclude this Lifestyle Tool, reflect on the following questions:

- What is the greatest challenge to practicing wise and kind speech at home or work?
- How can you use a security priming of soothing words to help become more at peace with challenges in your life?
- What words or stories would be in your security priming?
- What is one small way that you can be more transparent and genuine with your feelings?

∞

Chapter 8

PLANTING FRIENDSHIP SEEDS

Remember, the path is never as arduous as it looks —
only resistance makes it so.
Many teachers are walking among you now,
and you are a teacher to many.
You become the angelic messenger
when you send love to a stranger.

— Frank Coppieters, *Handbook for the Evolving Heart*

D o you have a favorite "buddy" movie? Almost every genre
has films that feature friendships, from horror, sports, and
westerns to sci-fi and animated children's stories. Here are a few
memorable TV and film friendships, which often show how op-
posites can overcome their conflicts to create enduring, loving
partnerships: *Star Trek*'s Captain Kirk (human) and Spock (Vul-
can); *Shaun of the Dead*'s Shaun (alive) and Ed (zombie); *Dumb
and Dumber*'s Harry (dumb) and Lloyd (yes, dumber); *Jerry
Maguire*'s Jerry (desperate sports agent) and Rod (greedy foot-
ball player); *Walking and Talking*'s Laura (getting married) and
Amelia (unhappily single); *Lethal Weapon*'s Murtaugh (family cop)
and Riggs (suicidal cop); *The Big Lebowski*'s Dude (mellow dude)
and Walter (wound-up guy); *The Odd Couple*'s Felix (uptight

clean freak) and Oscar (super slob); *Toy Story*'s Woody (traditional cowboy toy) and Buzz (futuristic toy); *Free Willy*'s Jesse (young boy) and Willy (Orca whale); and *Harry Potter*'s Hogwarts trio of Harry, Hermione, and Ron. Some of these pairings make the story of longtime friends CD and Hillary in *Beaches* appear downright mundane!

What all these movie friendships have in common is the deep bond and connection forged through life experience that only true friends share. With friends, you let down your guard and allow others to see the real you. While doing this can be scary, there are real benefits. But first, let's consider the opposite: What if we isolate and don't have friends or a support network? We may have good reasons for doing this, but how will that affect our life?

It turns out that isolation negatively affects our emotional and physical health. Research shows that *not* having a network of family or friends can be as bad for our health as being an alcoholic, smoking fifteen cigarettes a day, or being obese. A large meta-analytic review looked at 148 different studies (with over three hundred thousand participants) to examine how social relationships influenced health and mortality rate. The study, published in the journal *Public Library of Science Medicine*, concluded, "The influence of social relationships on risk is comparable with well-established risk factors for mortality." In fact, we have a 50 percent greater chance of living longer if we have strong social support.

Other studies indicate that as we age, friendship becomes even more critical. A study conducted in Australia, published in the *Journal of Epidemiology and Community Health*, followed more than fourteen hundred individuals who were at least seventy years old over a ten-year period. After controlling for variables like health and lifestyle, they found that an individual's social network acted as a protective factor, lengthening survival rates in the elderly.

If misery loves company, is the same true of happiness? Can

friendship affect our emotional state? It turns out that happiness not only loves company, it may actually be contagious. In the first study to investigate how emotions like happiness can spread indirectly, researchers from Harvard Medical School and the University of California, San Diego, used data to track over forty-five hundred individuals and their fifty thousand family and social connections. Happiness, they discovered, was spread through contact, much like catching a cold. The data showed that if one of our friends is happy, we have a 15.3 percent greater chance of being happy. And if our friend has a happy friend, that will increase our likelihood of being happy by 9.8 percent. Furthermore, happiness spreads more easily depending upon geographic proximity. If friends, siblings, and relatives live far away or in another city, this will have little effect on our happiness. Those who live closer to us have a greater effect. In addition, face-to-face contact produced a greater degree of happiness compared to contact with others using the phone or internet.

FRIENDSHIP'S NURTURING QUALITIES

Lloyd, a fifty-year-old man who came to see me for unresolved grief over the loss of his father, is one example of someone who was isolated and lonely. "I think about him all the time," Lloyd told me. Lloyd explained that as his father's health diminished, he devoted all his time to his father's care. Since his father lived hundreds of miles away, Lloyd caught the Friday evening red-eye flight so he could spend the weekend watching over him. On Sunday afternoon, he returned home. Lloyd did this for three years until his father passed away. I was very touched by this devoted and admirable act of compassion and caring, but the downside was that Lloyd steadily lost his own circle of friends. Lloyd now had a gaping hole in his social support network.

"In order to be with my father," he explained, "I stopped seeing my own friends. My father's friends, who were all older, became my friends. Some of them are gone now, too." After his father died, Lloyd spent the following three years isolated, other than going to work. Lloyd never restored his social network. We talked about how having friends and sharing stories of his father with others could help him step out of his grief. He agreed that would be helpful, but he didn't know where to start. Rather than re-create the wheel, I asked Lloyd how he had connected with others in the past. It turned out that he met friends through sports activities such as playing in an adult basketball league.

Together, we located several basketball leagues in his area. Lloyd later made calls to learn more. Once he got involved in activities outside of work, he started to develop new friendships. Reconnecting with others in a positive way helped Lloyd clear away his grief and move on. Friendships have the power to help us heal past wounds and losses.

✦

How do your friends add to your life? Let's take a moment to look inwardly and reflect on the friendships in your life — past and present. As you review the following list, notice which of these qualities make you feel happy, safe, and secure. Which friendships exhibit some or many of these qualities?

If you have had a treasured friendship that ended or changed in a painful way, see if you can surround yourself with a sense of self-compassion. In this way, you make space for your experience — for any sadness, hurt, or disappointment — and allow it in. This also helps acknowledge that new friendships are possible.

- Friends accept us as we are, despite our flaws and glaring differences.
- Friends can challenge us when we need to grow and learn.

- Friends value what we have to say.
- Friends share our special interests and bring out our best.
- Friends are genuinely happy for our success and growth.
- Friends listen to our secrets and don't judge us.
- Friends loyally stand at our side, in good times and bad.
- Friends care deeply about us.
- Friends are supportive of us and act as resources.
- Friends have our backs — and make us feel safe and protected.
- Friends can share their deepest feelings and emotions.
- Friendship can deepen over the years.
- Friends can be our mentors, guides, and teachers.
- Friends give us a sense of camaraderie and belonging.
- Friends help us feel alive and joyful by sharing life experiences.

Just taking time to explore your friendships requires the strength of personal insight. If you would like more friends, imagine yourself offering the qualities above to another. If there were a wise recipe for cultivating lasting and loving friendships through the act of giving — not taking — my vote would go to these selected lines from the Saint Francis prayer.

> Where there is hatred, let me sow love;
> where there is injury, pardon;
> where there is doubt, faith;
> where there is despair, hope;
> where there is darkness, light;
> where there is sadness, joy....
> Grant that I may not so much seek to be consoled as to
>   console;
> to be understood as to understand;
> to be loved as to love.
> For it is in giving that we receive.

THE THREE SEEDS OF FRIENDSHIP

For my first job out of college, I worked in the family business, which in all truth was not to my liking. It was clerical work, and the office was situated in downtown Chicago, a long drive on the freeway from the Northwest suburbs during rush hour. One of the few bright spots in the office was a man named Hugh. He was unlike anyone I'd ever met in my young life. He had come in as a consultant to revamp the company's creaky accounting system.

This was in the early days of computing, and Hugh was so enthusiastic and bubbling with energy about using computers to update the accounting process that it was contagious — but not to my father and his business partner. When Hugh advocated changing some of the traditional office practices, he was fought every step of the way. I felt badly for him. We'd go to lunch, and he'd share his vast experiences, such as when he had been the vice president of a major railroad. Though he was some thirty years my senior, Hugh and I became friends. He had a light spirit that buoyed me during a time when I felt lost and unsure of my future.

Hugh had come upon some tough times, including divorce and financial difficulties. I was still living at home and was saving up money in order to share an apartment with a college friend. Around that time, Hugh asked me for a loan of five hundred dollars. It was a lot of money for me, but I lent it to him. When I mentioned this to my father, his jaw dropped and he said, "You'll never see a dime. He's flat broke and owes me money that I'll probably never see." To make a long story short, Hugh repaid his debt to me as he had promised. He knew I needed it, and the thing is, I never for a minute doubted he'd pay me back. When my father found out Hugh repaid me, he was flabbergasted.

Yet at the same time, I was at peace with my decision to lend Hugh the money. As a friend, I accepted that Hugh would do his best to pay me back, and I could live with that. I acted out of compassion because my friend was in need. Looking back, I realize that Hugh and I had planted the three seeds of friendship — trust, acceptance, and empathy.

> LIFESTYLE TOOL: Plant the Seeds of Trust, Acceptance, and Empathy

Read each of the descriptions of the three seeds, then reflect on or answer the questions at the end of this Lifestyle Tool.

Seed of Trust

Trust is vital to any relationship because without it there *is* no relationship, no feeling of mutuality or safety. Here are three ways to grow trust.

1. **Listen to your gut.** Pay attention for any red flags, like a clenched-up feeling or a small question or doubt in your mind. If there's a warning signal that says you are not safe, you can always slow down until those doubts or questions get answered.

2. **Don't rush trust.** Trust takes time to grow. One reason people often get hurt in relationships is that they disclose too much about themselves far too soon, before they really know if the other person is trustworthy. In the therapy room, there are ethical guidelines for confidentiality that are designed to provide safety and trust for clients. In relationships, we need those guidelines, too, though they aren't spelled out on a Professional Disclosure Statement. A new friendship can be fun and exciting, but allow it to grow naturally. A large oak tree doesn't sprout overnight.

3. **Be honest and transparent.** Being honest doesn't mean hitting someone over the head with your personal version

of "truth." It means that you are genuine and not decep-
tive. It means that your friend can count on what you say
and do.

Seed of Acceptance

Acceptance is a second seed that nurtures friendships. Acceptance is very much an attitude that recognizes that no one is
perfect, not even your LOL BFF. Here are three guidelines for
developing acceptance.

1. **Notice frailties — your own and those of others —
   without being too harsh.** Acceptance doesn't mean
   that we accept abuse, but that we can be more forgiving
   and open. Acceptance means giving more space to your
   friends so they can feel accepted for just being themselves.

2. **Be supportive and express happiness for your friend.**
   Friendship is not a competition but a way of being supportive. Showing your joyfulness for the success of your
   friend is like being a mascot or cheerleader on the sidelines. This is the case even if your friend's choices happen
   to be ones you wouldn't choose for yourself.

3. **Practice forgiveness for those times when your friend
   may be less than perfect.** A friend may disappoint you
   but can still be a trusted friend. Forgiveness can take you
   beyond disappointment and anger, a wonderful way of
   learning to let go and let be.

Seed of Empathy

With empathy we can connect deeply with our friends. We can
feel their needs as well as share the range of emotions, from compassion to joy. Empathy is the gateway to intimacy, love, and

caring for another. Here are three methods for tapping the bonding power of empathy.

1. **Attune, link, and listen to your friend.** Aligning with another's emotional state and feelings lets us know what it's like to be in that person's shoes. If a friend is sad, allow yourself to connect by listening to the person's story and feeling his or her sadness rather than talking your friend out of it. Attunement develops closeness. Later, you can always rationally discuss your friend's emotions.

2. **Slow your breathing, and get into your body.** Breathing lets you get out of your head and get very present with your friend in the moment. To feel what another is feeling creates a very powerful bond of understanding.

3. **Let yourself be joyful with friends.** For some, friends become an easy target for talking about life complaints and worries. Yes, friends can help you deal with pain, but friendship is about sharing the full menu of life's emotions. As the wise sage and poet Rumi reminds us, "People want you to be happy. Don't keep serving them your pain!"

Now, ask yourself the following questions:

- In what ways have I succeeded in my friendships? What seeds work in making my friendships strong and enduring?
- Which of these seeds could help make my friendships more complete?
- What is one seed I could plant in an existing or new friendship?
- What is one small action I could take that would let my friends know I trust, accept, and have empathy for them?

∞

Chapter 9

FOR THE LOVE OF LISTENING

You can talk and talk, but the longer you talk, the worse it gets — the further you are from the truth.

— George Washington Carver

TV has an abundance of "talk shows" but no "listen shows." Both talking and listening are necessary for communicating, but for some reason, talking seems a lot sexier. In some sense, talking can be viewed as a form of taking. When you talk, you "grab" someone's attention. You "give" your opinion, rather than receive the opinions and thoughts of others. Great actors and speakers "take command" of the stage. Which do you think is more important — talking or listening? Which do you depend upon most? Which one makes you feel good?

Now, if we're honest, talking probably makes us feel better — especially if we're talking about ourselves. Look no further than Twitter or Facebook, where over 75 percent of all posts, according to some surveys, are broadcasts of one's immediate, subjective experiences. Researchers at Harvard wanted to understand this human need, and they used a combination of brain imaging and cognitive methods to understand what happens in the brain when we self-disclose. Participants in the study could make small amounts of money by talking about the opinions of another person, as well as neutral topics. Or they could lose this potential money by talking about their own opinions, feelings, and personal experiences. Published in the *Proceedings of the National Academy of Sciences*, the study found that people would rather talk about themselves than earn money. Why is talking about ourselves so satisfying? Researchers learned that self-disclosure stimulates the brain's pleasure, satisfaction, and reward system — the same system that gets turned on with food, sex, drugs, and money. And yet, talking alone does little to further understanding and true communication. Only by listening can we truly journey to the inner world of others.

What does it mean to *really, really listen*? George Washington Carver — who was like the Thomas Edison of the plant world — discovered more than three hundred uses for the peanut. Carver's secret tool was listening. He would wake up in the early morning, have a small breakfast, and by 4 a.m. be communing with the peanuts and other plants he was studying. "There are certain things," he said, "often very little things, like the little peanut, the little piece of clay, the little flower that cause you to look *within* — and then it is that you see into the soul of things."

As Carver learned, listening is not a passive activity. Listening is best done as a uni-tasking activity. In this way we mindfully, respectfully, and intentionally give our presence and attention to another. If we're only half-heartedly listening, such as tapping a text message or working on the computer while in a conversation, that's the equivalent of turning around and walking away from whoever is standing before us.

CLEARING CLUTTER TO LISTEN WELL

When we "see red" because of old reactive ruts — especially those triggered by the emotional clutter of people we know well — our brain's ability to listen shuts down. One example of this was Beth, a thirty-five-year-old woman who felt frequently criticized by her mother. "If I'm giving my kids space," she told me, "my mother accuses me of being neglectful. If I'm helping my kids with school or planning activities for them, she says I'm a helicopter mom. I just can't win."

Whenever her mother called, Beth's defenses went on high alert. She tensed up and often got upset or angry. Beth became a victim of her brain's survival wiring. That's because the brain is wired to react defensively to *any* threat, including a perceived threat or even a threat to our ego. (Of course, if we were less attached to our ego needs, we would have less reason to get defensive.)

To understand this, we need to understand how the brain processes what we hear. Sound travels from the auditory nerve to the verbal processing center in the brain — known as Wernicke's area. But first, the brain's smoke detector (the amygdala) receives that input. Remember, the amygdala intercepts what's coming in from all our senses — sight, sound, touch, taste, smell, and even the orienting muscles in our neck — in order to sniff out anything that is potentially threatening. For Beth, hearing criticism from her mother triggered her defense system, which in turn impaired her ability to listen and respond in the moment.

Why are we hardwired this way? It makes perfect sense when you consider our early evolutionary history — when automatically responding to the sound of a tiger growling in the jungle might save your life. Today, our survival system doesn't know the difference between an argument, a job review, a contentious staff meeting, a critical comment — or a hungry tiger.

To help Beth overcome her hardwiring, I gave her four simple instructions. These were designed to help her derail the old clutter rut that turned on her defense system and kept her from listening. Using this method she could listen beneath the content of the words in order to grasp a fresh meaning from her mother's communication.

1.   **Drop all assumptions about the person for this conversation.** I asked Beth to intentionally let go of her old wiring and ruts for the duration of her conversation. She could always go back to them later.

2.   **Tune in to the emotional subtext of another's words by paying attention to tone of voice, body language, gestures, and facial expressions.** The reason for this was that I wanted Beth not to get stuck on the content of what her mother was saying, but to get to the deeper feeling of what was really being expressed.

3.   **Get curious about the person you are communicating with.** I wanted Beth to break her old rut of familiarity by imagining she was speaking with an interesting stranger. By experiencing her mother as if she were meeting her for the first time, Beth could let go of expectation and take the experience less personally.

4.   **Notice if your thoughts about the person are accurate or automatic.** The purpose for this was to help Beth create some constructive distance from her thoughts as well as learn to appraise them. By judging the accuracy of her thoughts in the moment, she was preparing herself to change course, rather than responding automatically.

When Beth came back into the office, she gave me a very different perspective about her mother: "I heard something very different when talking with her. I heard loneliness. I think she's trying to connect with me, but she doesn't know how. It made me sad to see how lonely she is. For the first time in a long time, I felt compassion for her."

By doing the exercise above, Beth learned the important

mindfulness skill of metacognition — reflecting inwardly to appraise her thoughts and judgments. Metacognition has long been recognized in the field of education as a means by which we learn. With metacognition we can analyze our thinking — rather than jump to conclusions. This mindfulness ability lets us take a step back and create space from our thoughts.

In the context of listening, metacognition gives us constructive distance from reactivity. It buys us time by letting us review *how* we're thinking about something. For example, by detecting an inaccuracy in our appraisal of a situation or conversation, we can change course on the fly. We might decide to ask a clarifying question or even challenge our own automatic thinking.

Have you ever experienced robotic, conditioned thinking? So-called snap judgments happen so quickly that we skip the step of reflecting and reappraising. Personally, I recall a time when a fellow therapist and friend asked me about the possibility of writing a book with him. I responded in knee-jerk fashion with a quick no. But a moment of reflection helped me recognize the reflexive, robotic response. Right then and there, I apologized for my quick answer and asked him to share the idea. Thanks to mindful reflection, I was able to listen and be fully present and escape my own conditioned clutter.

SURRENDERING TO DEEPER UNDERSTANDING

If you want to become full,
let yourself be empty.
If you want to be reborn,
let yourself die.

— Lao Tzu, *Tao Te Ching*, translated by Stephen Mitchell

How full is your cup when talking with another? If your cup is overflowing with your own opinions, thoughts, and ideas, there may be no more room for what others have to share or contribute. Have you ever tried to share something with someone whose cup was too filled for them to hear you? The skill of listening is an ancient art. It was fine-tuned through a contemplative practice originally used by the desert monks in the second and third centuries. The practice, called Lectio Divina, was a way to empty your cup and surrender yourself to new and deeper ways of receiving, listening, and understanding. While the strict translation means "divine reading," Lectio Divina is really about divine listening.

Lectio Divina is about surrendering our old beliefs to gain a more profound understanding of our story and the stories of others. Sacred reading, or any contemplative listening practice, changes how we experience our stories. Through any meaningful writing, scripture, poetry, or image, we surrender our rational and preconditioned thinking in order to open to a process of discovery. The process typically includes reading a short passage over and over — slowing narrowing focus to a short phrase or word that speaks to the reader — until a deeper meaning is revealed. It is this revealed understanding that takes you on a journey to the unexplored parts of your story. The reading is sometimes followed by a process of inquiry, such as asking yourself, "What did I see or hear? What do I need to do with my new knowledge?"

Ultimately, Lectio Divina brings a sense of acceptance and peace to your own story, as well as our shared stories. Native Americans, such as the Navajo, use ceremonies, dances, and paintings to heal and create this same sense of exploration and harmony. Any of us can learn to listen in this kind of sacred way. Emptying our cups of preconceived and judgmental thoughts allows us to refill our cups a few savory drops at a time, making sure to always leave space. The Lifestyle Tool that follows brings together the ideas in this chapter, giving you a daily practice for listening more deeply and compassionately.

LIFESTYLE TOOL: How Do You HEAR?

We need new ways of freely listening and communicating that help us remain open, creative, and compassionate. Whatever clutter may be getting in your way during a conversation or communication, use the simple acronym HEAR to enter a more spacious and less defensive awareness. HEAR stands for: hold all assumptions; enter the emotional world; absorb and accept; and reflect, then respect.

H — Hold All Assumptions

To truly enter into a space of openness with another, it's important to let go of your previously held assumptions. Empty your ego, and be curious. Empty your cup of mental clutter and opinions, even if you feel personally criticized. Letting go of assumptions means that you are on an objective fact-finding mission. It doesn't mean that you can't still advocate for yourself or protect yourself. Take an attitude of curiosity toward this person — how did he or she develop these ideas? What concerns does the person have? Is he or she speaking from a place of fear or worry?

E — Enter the Emotional World

What happens when you push against someone's mood or beliefs? Suppose you tell an angry person, "It's silly to be angry. I'm not listening to a word you're saying. It's not helping. You can think better when you calm down."

Instead of giving an answer, a demand, or a command, which could be enraging, try empathetically entering that person's emotional world. Entering means joining with them for a moment and feeling what it's like to be in their shoes. You might respond, "I've never seen you this angry [or sad, upset, frustrated, and so on]. Can you help me understand? I'd really like to know how you feel so we can work on solving the problem." Empathy is akin to the martial arts practice of jujitsu, which uses the energy of an opponent to disarm them, rather than directly opposing the person. In brain science terms, empathy gives a hug to an upset person's amygdala.

In addition, pay attention to the emotional subtext or meaning. As you notice body language, gestures, and vocal tone, allow yourself to make a mental representation of what this feels like. Is there an insight or something unsaid that you might express? By entering another's world, you are more able to successfully engage with that person.

A — Absorb and Accept

Do you know the "telephone game," where a phrase or sentence is whispered to successive people in a circle? By the time the phrase makes its way to the final person, it usually bears little or no resemblance to the original statement. It's easy to misinterpret what we hear, and that's why we need to absorb what someone says to us by listening with understanding and openness.

Think of how a sponge absorbs water on a countertop. The sponge doesn't just slosh the water around from one place to another. Absorbing another's point of view often requires time. It means asking clarifying questions. Absorption is a process of listening, understanding, questioning, and then rephrasing in your own words to make certain you understand.

We might be able to absorb what another says, but without acceptance, the absorption won't stick. Acceptance is necessary for us to surrender to another's perspective. Acceptance doesn't mean we must agree, but we remain open to how another feels.

R — Reflect, Then Respect

Reflection is the metacognitive step of pausing and looking inward to think about what you have heard. You may not be ready to respond right away, and it's okay to pause. Reflection is a step where you allow for space and openness in order to listen to your inner wisdom and kindness. Sometimes a long walk without trying to get an answer is the way to reflect. Sharing your concerns with a wise benefactor might also help you reflect.

When you are ready to respond, do so respectfully and with kindness. Don't respond when you feel angry. When your heart is filled with wisdom and love and respect, that is the time to speak and respond.

∞

Chapter 10

EXPANDING YOUR TRIBE

A human being is a part of the whole, called by us "Universe," a part limited in time and space. He experiences himself, his thoughts and feelings, as something separated from the rest — a kind of optical delusion of his consciousness. This delusion is a kind of prison for us....Our task must be to free ourselves from this prison by widening our circle of compassion to embrace all living creatures and the whole of nature in its beauty.

— Albert Einstein

Before city-states developed, humans organized themselves into social groups we call tribes. Today's tribes can be thought of as any group that you bond with and that shares a set of social values. In this context, tribes (or groups) can signify your family, a close-knit group of friends, a political or religious affiliation, and even a workplace culture. What "tribes" do you strongly identify and connect with? We don't always choose our tribes, and sometimes we take on a tribe's worldview as if it were gospel.

Take a moment to consider how your groups, or tribes, view outsiders. Do they view those with opposing viewpoints with suspicion? Are they open and accepting of outsiders? How do your loyalties and obedience to the tribe — the family tribe, the cultural tribe, the blog tribe, the friend tribe, the country tribe, and the workplace tribe — influence your worldview?

Have you ever heard of the term "imprinting"? Animals such as baby ducks, goslings, and chicks bond with their parents at a very young age. They are programmed to follow the first moving object in their world — typically, their mother — everywhere it goes. The process is called "imprinting," and it is how the youngster learns important survival skills. Scientists have long known that birds will imprint on humans or even objects like dolls or sticks.

Imprinting and bonding with family and other groups serves an important purpose in helping us survive. But what if your tribe is limited in the lessons it offers you? Take the events dramatized in the film *Fly Away Home*, in which a flock of orphaned Canada goose chicks were adopted by a human family — and imprinted on them. The humans soon learned, unfortunately, that their goose "family" would not survive the winter. That's because young geese depend on older "mentors" who know the migratory route and teach it to the newbies. To compensate for this loss, the geese were taught to follow a low-speed ultralight aircraft, which led the birds from Ontario, Canada, to Virginia. In real life, pilot Bill Lishman actually did this, teaching geese to migrate using an ultralight aircraft, and the birds, having learned the path once, successfully managed the migratory trip on their own in the following years.

DECODING YOUR TRIBE'S MESSAGES

Without doubt, our various tribes outline a road map of what it means to be successful and what personal traits are desirable. Sometimes this happens explicitly; media, laws, pop culture, and organizations define acceptable conduct and values. Sometimes the messages are subtle. A few years back, I sat next to a Japanese-born business professor on an airplane trip. He was returning from taking a group of MBA students from a prestigious East Coast business school on a trip to Texas. There, they visited a highly successful computing company. The company's motto, he explained, was "Winning Culture." The Japanese professor felt that the motto was too one-sided and that it ignored the importance of collaboration with others. He felt there needed to be more of a balance and less of an us-versus-them approach. Clearly, though, the Texas company's message is embedded in Western culture.

It's natural to get imprinted by the beliefs of our culture, institutions, and families. What's most important, however, is that you understand what viewpoint matters most to you. For example, just because your family tribe taught you "never to cry" as a child doesn't mean you have to bottle up your emotions as an adult. Just because you had a sports coach who taught you to "win at all costs" doesn't mean that life is a black-and-white, win-or-lose proposition.

Right now, give yourself a pat on the back for investigating these ideas. Perhaps the bigger question is this: How inclusive, or exclusive, is your tribal view? Does it allow you, as Einstein said, to widen your "circle of compassion to embrace all living creatures and the whole of nature in its beauty"? Does it encourage a limited *me* perspective — or does it encourage a more tolerant, forgiving, and accepting *we* perspective? Does your perspective allow for respecting and making space for those who are different than you?

The good news is that no one is permanently wedded to a particular clan or tribe. You can always create your own tribe, your own group of like-minded, open, and compassionate individuals. This is, perhaps, how you can begin to shape the world into a more inclusive and caring place.

WINNING TOGETHER:
COMMUNICATING THROUGH DIALOGUE

See yourself in others.
Then whom can you hurt?
What harm can you do?

— Buddha, *The Dhammapada*

Did you ever have a discussion with someone about religion or politics, but you just couldn't see eye to eye? Even though you might have had respect for that person, it's likely that the chasm between your views remained as wide as the Grand Canyon. Why do people avoid discussing political and religious topics? It's not the topics themselves that are volatile, but how attached and loyal we are to our tribe's views.

Sports teams are good examples of tribes that we strongly identify with. I recall the time I went to see the Trail Blazers, Portland's professional basketball team, with my friend Jeff. The Blazers won, and walking back to the car, I noticed how happy Jeff and I were because of our team's victory. Of course, that meant that there were unhappy Denver Nuggets fans. I felt sympathy for the Denver fans, but the Nuggets players weren't really losers — they probably went home to nice houses with lots of amenities. Nonetheless, I posed this question to Jeff: What would it be like if there were more cooperation between teams — thus no winner and no loser? We laughed at this idea and decided that would be the end of all sports. Sports depends on our closeness and attachment to a particular team or city. We identify strongly, and as a result, we want to see our team do well. They are our tribe.

Team sports, thankfully, also offer us an important counterbalancing lesson. They demonstrate over and over that the team with only one superstar cannot win. Even a team with two selfish superstars won't win. Michael Jordan didn't win alone; he needed a team. Winning is only one measure of team success — being part of a team is energizing and motivating. It's a metaphor for how we share, communicate, care, and include others.

Likewise, if we want to be a successful planet, we need to include other tribes in our circle. One intriguing path for doing this has been explored by physicist David Bohm and others. It is called *dialogue*, which translated means "through word." Essentially, dialogue is a process of letting go of needing our team to finish first. It's a process that asks us to dig into our past to see what assumptions — cultural or otherwise — are blocking us from finding a place of common understanding with another. In *On Dialogue*, Bohm writes:

> People have difficulty communicating even in small groups....Why is that? For one thing, everybody has different assumptions and opinions. They are basic assumptions — not merely superficial assumptions — such as assumptions about the meaning of life; about your own self-interest, your country's interest, or your religious interest; about what you really think is important. And these assumptions are defended when they are challenged. People frequently can't resist defending them, and they tend to defend them with an emotional charge....
>
> The point is that dialogue has to go into all the pressures that are behind our assumptions. It goes into the process of thought *behind* the assumptions, not just the assumptions themselves.

One of the key components of dialogue is exploring what are called "absolute necessities." These are those beliefs that are most deeply embedded in how we think and feel. What often causes conflicts between different tribes — such as cultures, religions, and so on — is that each of us clings to very different and clashing absolute necessities. Sometimes, these necessities are hidden factors driving a conflict. Here are examples of opposing absolute necessities:

- Culture A's absolute necessity supports freedom of speech as the core foundation for constitutional democracy and freedom of expression.
- Culture B's absolute necessity supports censorship on media that is considered to be immoral or insensitive to others.
- Culture C's absolute necessity supports adherence to time promptness; otherwise, one is untrustworthy, disrespectful, and disorganized.
- Culture D's absolute necessity supports effort, preparation, and passion. Being a slave to the clock is meaningless and shows lack of creativity.

I recall the time that a friend of mine started dating on the internet. When I asked about his first coffee date, he initially thought it went well. There was a good feeling on both sides, he explained, and they had arranged for another date. Then he remembered that his date didn't adhere to his political beliefs. He canceled the next day because of his absolute necessity.

In workshops, I've asked individuals to consider their absolute necessities, and many individuals do not want to look in that direction. Imagine the dialogue between someone whose absolute necessity was a belief in God, while another's absolute necessity was atheism, the belief that there is no God. It can be frightening to think about letting go of something that feels so much a part of who we are, but no one said it was easy clearing out emotional clutter.

The benefit of looking at what is blocking you from including and working with others in your life — and the willingness to let it go, even temporarily — is that this can do the heavy lifting of clearing out hidden emotional obstructions. Bohm was not naïve, and while he worked to promote an understanding of dialogue, he also knew that it requires a long-term commitment from both sides.

We can't control whether other people will be tolerant and willing to let go of their absolute necessities. Fortunately, there seems to be an important factor that can transcend the identification we have with our tribe — which can increase compassion for outsiders. A study published in *Psychological Science* found that individuals with an intense allegiance or loyalty to a group did not automatically reject those in other groups. The moderating factor was one's moral beliefs. Researchers discovered that individuals who had genuine moral beliefs had fewer aggressive impulses toward outsiders. Using different scenarios, the study demonstrated those with a strong moral identity were more likely to condemn torture as well as share a limited supply of food with strangers. The takeaway message is a hopeful one. A deep sense of morality is a useful way to realize that we are all, ultimately, members of the same team. And while we cannot control others, broadening our understanding and releasing our own absolute necessities is a big step in the right direction.

Dialogue is simply one path to reducing intolerance in the world. Tolerance also grows from a basic understanding about the nature of suffering and how all things are interconnected. This knowing can transcend language and dialogue. It can be like a second sight, a penetrating awareness that Vietnamese Buddhist monk, author, and teacher Thich Nhat Hanh often referred to as *interbeing*.

> If you are a poet, you will see clearly that there is a cloud floating in this sheet of paper. Without a cloud, there will be no rain; without rain, the trees cannot grow; and without trees we cannot make paper. The cloud is essential for the paper to exist. If the cloud is not here, the sheet of paper cannot be here either. So we can say that the cloud and the paper inter-are.... Looking even more deeply, we can see we are in it, too. This is not difficult to see, because when we look at a sheet of paper, the sheet of paper

is part of our perception. Your mind is in here and mine is also.... Everything coexists with this sheet of paper.... To be is to inter-be. You cannot just be by yourself alone.

The Lifestyle Tool that follows is another way to widen our compassionate circle and bring all beings and suffering ones inside.

LIFESTYLE TOOL: Experience Interbeing to Dissolve Differences between Tribes

We hold the innate potential for realizing connectedness. The experience of interbeing shrinks all our obvious differences — habits, politics, gender, age, religion, and culture — down into the realm of the insignificant. It affirms our commonality and dissolves the preoccupations that unnecessarily divide us.

To view things in this connected way means that when any one person is harmed, shamed, or humiliated, all of us suffer the same indignities. This awareness cultivates empathy and frees up compassion for the larger web of relationships. May we all practice interbeing to nourish greater understanding, love, and care for all beings. Take a few moments to answer the questions below as a reflective practice for expanding your felt connections with others.

- How has the pain of loss touched those you know, even those you don't know personally?
- How does the universality of loss help you find compassion for all people and beings?
- Who has helped you through difficult times in your life, through either listening, compassion, or action?
- What absolute necessity do you possess that separates you from others?

Finally, for a few minutes each day, allow yourself to notice and appreciate how everything depends on everything else, even in a subtle way.

∞

—— *Part 3* ——

Preventing New Emotional Clutter with Daily De-cluttering

Mindfulness acts like a guard at your door, blocking the never-ending onrush of emotional disregulation, disharmony, and dis-ease that demand entry to your life and your mind. In this section you will gain the confidence and the skills necessary to buffer daily stressors. You will feel the difference in your mental and physical well-being as you scrub away clutter in order to immerse yourself daily in peace, fulfillment, and joy.

Chapter 11

CHANGE THE DISTRACTION CHANNEL TO FIND CLARITY

A child born today is practically never away from the sixty-cycle hum, day or night. It is characteristic of every fluorescent light, every motor, every electronic device.... Such labor-saving devices should contribute to our contentment, but in the process of becoming skilled at controlling external reality, we often lose contact with inner realities.
— Robert Johnson and Jerry Ruhl, *Contentment*

Have you ever used technology and lost track of time? The engaging nature of computers, smartphones, TVs, and other visual technology creates a virtual hamster wheel that consumes our mind — keeping it busy and feeling in control. According to anthropologist Natasha Dow Schull, author of *Addiction by Design*, this is similar to what drives another kind of screen obsession — slot machine gambling. "When gamblers play," explained Schull in an interview with *New Republic*, "they're going into a zone that feels comfortable and safe. You're not playing to win, you're playing to stay in the zone — a zone where all of your daily worries, your bodily pains, your anxieties about money and time and relationships, fall away."

As a zone and buffer against anxiety and worry, media and

technology may seem preferable to medications like Xanax or Prozac. But there's a dark side to media distraction. It can steal away hours of time and fill our minds with all kinds of unwanted static. The result is that we may lose focus on what we'd find really fulfilling and joyful. In some cases, media distraction can affect our moods and behavior.

The American Psychological Association investigated the effects of media and technology through three comprehensive reports: the Task Force on Advertising and Children, the Task Force on Violence in Video Games and Interactive Media, and the Task Force on the Sexualization of Girls. The latter task force found that exposure to pervasive sexualizing and objectifying images produced problems in key areas: cognitive deficits and lack of confidence; mental health issues related to low self-esteem, eating disorders, and negative moods; unhealthy sexual attitudes and body acceptance; and skewed attitudes and beliefs about femininity and the importance of physical attractiveness. This clutter of daily media affects both women and men, as well as society at large, by influencing our roles and stereotypes. How have these major sources of daily static shaped your own life and experiences?

INTENTION:
THE ALL-PURPOSE DISTRACTION CLEANSER

If you often feel driven to distraction and powerless to stem the tide of media and multitasking in your life, worry not. That's because you possess one of the most powerful quantum tools in the universe — something technology can't duplicate. You can engage this ultimate power tool to scrub away distraction, no matter how much this clutter wants to fill up the nooks and crannies of your life.

Such is the power of intention, from which comes your innate ability to manifest your very desires and actions in the world. Mental intention sets the world in motion. As one of the PAIR UP mindfulness skills, intention contains the seed of potential that, when nurtured, becomes reality. It can literally grow new synaptic connections and rewire your brain to remove emotional barriers when you get stuck.

Each action you make, however large or small, and whether conscious or not, is the result of a quantum environment in the brain. That's because each intention moves tiny charged particles (ions) into our neurons. When the charge of the ions becomes large enough, it causes that particular neural pathway to fire. That means that your intentions change your brain structure over time, which in turn changes how you think. Intention is the essence of free will.

Intentions act like the steering wheel of your vehicle; they turn you in a particular direction. If your life is in a rut, or keeps getting stuck in the same rut, then you need to look at how this keeps happening. How do distractions derail your intentions, letting them become dulled, robotic, or automated? To let distractions, inner or outer, determine your intentions, is to relinquish what makes you most human.

We don't always realize that we are in control of the negative behavior patterns in our life. One day, a client and I were exploring why the client kept repeating the same negative pattern, and he shrugged his shoulders and exclaimed, "By some weird mistake and accident, I've become the person I am!" A mistake and accident? Really? This man had relinquished control of his life. He just wasn't ready to take accountability for how he was letting his intentions and thoughts be hijacked by old conditioning and distracting stimuli. If you are not paying attention, you might be totally surprised to find yourself once again in that old, familiar ditch. But it's not an accident. The more you listen to and are aware of your intentions — even the tiny ones — the greater freedom you have to shape and determine your life's course.

Understanding intention is easy, and you can think of it like this:

If your intention is to grow an oak tree, don't spread mental dandelion seeds.

In the film *The History of the World, Part 1*, Mel Brooks, in the role of the French monarch, says the funny line, "It's good to be the king." The joke, obviously, is that while this is good for the king, it isn't much good for anyone else. It's bad to be a servant or a slave — of media, technology, or any master or monarch who abuses his or her power to steal away your free will.

Besides consuming time, tech clutter might even change the wiring of our brains and hijack our intentions — one of the most priceless gifts that we possess. Music, videos, games, films, news, and even emerging virtual technologies exert more influence than we realize, and we aren't even aware of it. Internet porn addiction, for example, is such a huge problem that sexual addiction specialist Dr. Ted Roberts, author of *Pure Desire*, refers to the internet as "crack cocaine for sexual addiction."

◆

For Roger, a successful, young executive, the clutter of mental static and confusion produced by media and technology was devastating. When he came to see me, his life was on the verge of falling apart due to internet porn addiction. It started innocuously enough, he told me, when his wife got a job working an evening shift at a manufacturing plant. "I didn't really want to be alone, and I got this bad feeling when she left. So I looked at adult porn for maybe five minutes that first night after she left the house, and it distracted me." That five minutes soon turned into thirty minutes, an hour, three hours, and seven hours a night while his wife was working. Before Roger knew it, he was addicted to this behavior, almost by "accident," since he'd never intended to become addicted to porn. The behavior led to some other related, risky behavior, and when his wife found out, she wanted a divorce.

In our work together, one thing I did was to ask Roger to write down his deepest values — in the form of an intention statement — for his relationship and marriage and to share this with his wife. I also asked him to create a list of positive behaviors that were compatible and congruent with his deepest desires. In the end, his intention was to create a relationship based on mutual love, respect, trust, honesty, compassion, and transparency. Watching porn was not congruent with any of that.

I also had Roger sit and be present with the "bad feeling" he was trying to avoid when he was alone in the house. He didn't want to do this, but it helped him discover a painful, old feeling of abandonment that he experienced in childhood — when his parents would argue violently and one or both would suddenly leave the house. After Roger gained a new understanding of his fear of being alone, his need to avoid that feeling disappeared as well.

How to Exercise Free Will (and Free Won't)

Intention is truly a powerful engine of free will. It links us to the insight and lessons from past experience and choices; it links us to this present moment and our desire to move in a new direction; and it links us to our future, which we are intimately involved in manifesting. What is more, intentions are occurring even if we're not thinking about them. Let's take a moment to bring this down to the real world with the following questions. Ask yourself:

- How frequently and without even thinking do I seek out screen time on my smartphone, computer, TV, laptop, tablet, or game console?
- How frequently do I attend to technology when I could be present — face-to-face — with someone who is right beside me?
- How much time do I spend sitting on the couch watching someone else be active instead of participating in my own life?
- How does technology time cut into other activities I have enjoyed in the past?

There are no right or wrong answers to these questions. They are a point of personal investigation and inquiry as you begin to take a more proactive approach to tech clutter.

In *The Mindful Brain*, psychiatrist Daniel Siegel wrote, "Intentions create an integrated state of priming, a gearing up of our neural system to be in the mode of that specific intention: we can be readying to receive, to sense, to focus, to behave in a certain manner. Intention is not just about motor action....Intention is a central organizing process in the brain that creates continuity beyond the present moment."

When I was in the monastery, much of the mindfulness work the monks practiced was around using intentionality during basic daily activities like eating and walking. When eating, we set intentions for each movement — lifting the fork, opening the mouth, chewing the food, swallowing, and so on. When practicing walking, we set the intention to lift the foot, move it forward, set it down, and even shift the weight from one side of the body to the other. There wasn't any time for multitasking! When we walked, we walked. When we ate, we ate. When we sat, we sat. This was *uni-tasking*, a powerful way to be intentional in the moment and break out of old ruts and habits.

This might seem like an odd way to practice with intention, but the purpose was to make us aware of all the little things over which we had control. It took us off autopilot and put the inner robot on hold. Personally, it made me acutely aware of how easily the robot could take over at any time. Not all intentions are equally effective, and I learned that intentions work best when they are phrased proactively and positively — as opposed to intentions that express what you don't want in your life.

Here's an example of a negatively phrased intention: "I don't want to be numbed out by technology and not be present with those around me." Because it's stating what you *don't* want, it doesn't tell you how to behave in order to be more alive and in tune with the moment. So as an experiment, follow these instructions for adopting the intention to be fully present in this moment:

> Right now, as you read this sentence, set the mental intention to be fully present with all your senses. Then look to the right and to the left. Feel your neck and head as you turn in both directions. Notice what this feels like in the neck muscles. Observe closely the colors, shapes, and objects that you see. Listen to any sounds in the environment.

Hopefully, this very simple, proactive intention accomplished its goal, leading you to be aware and in touch with your body and this moment. Admittedly, it was a small moment, but it was filled with life and presence! In fact, you can be present using technology by setting similar intentions to notice your fingers on the computer keyboard, to notice the colors on the screen, and to be aware of your breath. In this way, you are not hypnotized; you are present even as you engage with technology. With this awareness, you can decide when you are in a state of distraction or overload and need to step back.

These moment-to-moment intentions help us bring our full presence to whatever we're doing. There are also larger value-oriented life intentions, or meta-intentions. These are the vital choices that direct our life and clear away distracting clutter. Author Deepak Chopra defined intention this way: "Intention is not simply a whim. It requires attention, and it also requires detachment. Once you've created the intention mindfully, you must be able to detach from the outcome, and let the universe handle the details of fulfillment."

Meta-intentions wake us up to our deeper purpose. They help us feel alive and connect us to the desire for love, wellness, health, connection, and balance. Meta-intentions are most powerful when stated affirmatively and when they include the word "choose." For instance, rather than saying, "I must lose weight to be healthy," this intention could be phrased proactively as "I choose to be healthier by eating more unprocessed foods and taking a walk each day." Instead of stating, "I want to be less influenced by technology and media," a positively phrased intention might be "I choose to build relationships by unplugging and focusing on face-to-face connections with people whenever possible."

In these positively phrased statements, not only are you specifying what you will do, rather than what you won't, but you emphasize that you're making a choice. This is a gentle reminder that you are deliberately choosing to turn in a particular direction. You don't have to do this, but you choose to do so.

When you have a positive meta-intention, write it down. This can be an intention for your relationships, for career, for friendship, or for financial security. Keep it somewhere that you can look at it throughout the day — such as on your cell phone or on a card you carry in your purse or wallet. Each time you look at it, breathe it into your being and absorb it into the cells of your body. Feel yourself connect with the benefits of your meta-intention.

Keep in mind that meta-intentions aren't finished products; it is best to let go of expectations and outcome. Attachment to an outcome is really another form of suffering. Let yourself experience the present-moment thoughts and deeds that grow from your intention. Let yourself be surprised at how these may manifest. Because of the nature of interbeing and connectedness, recognize how your intentions transcend selfishness and are good for all.

Another way to use intention is to use your brain's veto power, or *free won't*. Brain researcher Benjamin Libet, author of *Mind Time*, studied this ability. According to Libet, we can stop automatic or robotic behavior through exercising this inner veto power. Libet wrote, "The existence of a veto possibility is not in doubt. The subjects in our experiments at times reported that a conscious wish or urge to act appeared but that they suppressed or vetoed it." Have you ever had an unhealthy urge that you stopped or suppressed? Maybe you wanted that extra cookie or to buy something you really didn't need. Maybe you imposed the internal stop sign on the urge to get angry or say an unkind word — pausing and waiting until you calmed down, knowing this served you better. Because the brain works very quickly, it can jump in and impose the veto even as you are ready to act impulsively.

Each time you exercise free will and free won't, you strengthen the intentionality circuits in your brain. You increase your ability to pause and reflect inwardly and then to choose the beneficial or healthy direction you want to take. Start small, with more intentionality as you go through your day. Be aware of how you stand in the morning, of how you take a shower. Be more intentional as you get dressed and button your shirt, as you prepare and eat your food. Of course, many small actions become automatic. We do them "mindlessly," on autopilot, and this isn't necessarily failure or a bad thing. But when we find ourselves spinning on that virtual hamster wheel — then we know there's a problem. Our intentions and choices are failing to express what is really important to us.

Today, technology is a necessary part of our lives. However, even if we can't avoid technology, we can become aware of its impact as a sometimes hidden force, profoundly influencing how we live, how we think, and how we interact socially. For instance, many people find that frequent multitasking on tech devices reduces their ability to concentrate for sustained periods of time. In response, there are now "slow reading groups" — in which people get together at cafés or other locations, turn off all electronic devices, and read their favorite books in silence, together. This is a wonderful example of harnessing intention and clarity in a static-filled world.

LIFESTYLE TOOL: Mindful Exploration of Time Spent

Have you ever inventoried how you actually spend your time? The purpose of the following exercise is to bring some clarity and explore (without judgment) how you allocate your time. Make a copy of this chart, and use it to estimate the time spent each day for each category — in half-hour increments. If you find overlap between categories, do the best you can to choose the most accurate category. The idea here is to augment your awareness of how you are spending your time throughout the day and week, instead of mindlessly tuning in to distraction.

Activity	Time spent (in half-hour increments)						
	SUN.	MON.	TUES.	WED.	THURS.	FRI.	SAT.
Self-Care (Food, nutrition, and hygiene)							
Face-to-Face Conversation (Uninterrupted time with partner, friends, and family)							
Technology Use Not for Work or School (TV, CD, smartphone, DVD, email, video games, Facebook, and so on)							
Exercise (Physical activity of any kind)							
Spending Time in Nature							
Hobbies							
Travel and Scheduling (Planning, organizing, transitions)							
Reflection (Meditation, reading, personal growth and exploration)							
Work, School, and Study							
Desire and Cravings (Browsing and shopping)							
Sleep and Rest							

Ask yourself, and reflect on, these important questions:

- How do I feel about the current distribution of time spent? What surprises me most?
- What challenges, if any, does this distribution present me with?
- How does my use of technology affect other activities I have enjoyed in the past — such as reading an entire book, riding a bike, or other physical activities, and so on?
- How could I begin to redistribute my time in ways that would be more fulfilling and in line with my deeper values?
- What is one small, proactive intentional change I could make? (Write this down, and carry it with you, specifying the behavior that puts this intention into action.)
- What is a larger meta-intention that is related to my use of time and energy? (Again, write this down, and see how it affects your life and relationships.)

∞

Chapter 12

VACCINATE YOURSELF
AGAINST AFFLUENZA

Wisps of steam rise from the kettle. The simmering water sounds like the wind as it blows through the pines.... In the stillness wafts the fragrance of the tea.

— Soshitsu Sen XV, *Tea Life, Tea Mind*

Newness is enticing. Who doesn't enjoy that "new car smell"? Even now, I can vividly recall those times as a young boy when my father arrived home to announce he had a new automobile. The family would scramble outside for a look before excitedly climbing in for that first ride — often to the local ice cream shop. We would be in awe over this new shiny car. It was a special moment, and we were sure that this new car was way better than the old one, which would never be seen again. That was my introduction into America's car culture, as well as to the enticing power of newness and the rewarding feeling that can come from having more.

Plato used the word *pharmakon* to represent something that was simultaneously a poison and a remedy. The unquenchable craving for more and the desire for newness might be considered a pharmakon to some extent. Advertisers would like us to believe that whatever we own is outmoded and obsolete, not to mention old, worn-out, and no longer in style. Besides, isn't it better to have something new, bright, and shiny — something that improves how we feel and makes us more appealing to others? This all begs the question, When is enough really enough? When does novelty, newness, and the craving for more become counterproductive and reach the tipping point of becoming a pharmakon?

Daily clutter caused by the *more-bug* can be viewed as a socially contagious form of angst that is much like a virus or the flu. You catch the more-bug similar to the way that you catch a cold — by coming into direct or indirect contact with someone or something carrying the virus. If this more-bug takes hold, you can be overwhelmed by the unbridled desire for more, as well as consumed with anxiety and worry over not having enough. When, or if, this sickness reaches the equivalent of getting pneumonia or a serious infection, emergency intervention is required.

✦

Gwen was the poster child for someone infected with an acute case of the more-bug. Gwen came to see me for depression, and during our first session, she wept uncontrollably as she shared with me how she was holding on to the last vestiges of a life lived large. She was struggling to maintain appearances despite being in the midst of a personal hurricane: a divorce, a custody battle over her only child, and a looming financial crisis. She was then secretly sleeping in the vacant condo she and her husband had once owned — located near the mountains by a chic ski resort — but which was in the process of being repossessed by the bank. The furniture was gone, the electricity had been turned off, and Gwen slept on the floor in the living room rather than move in with her aging mother. She refused to stop driving her big, luxury SUV, which was also being repossessed. Sadly, Gwen defined herself by how she dressed, what kind of car she drove, and where she lived.

When I asked her to describe what happened to her marriage, Gwen answered, "I was so caught up in maintaining our lifestyle that I didn't realize that I no longer loved Curtis. We were going through the motions of being this successful, married couple. But there was no respect or love."

In one sense, Gwen got divorced and lost all her material goods due to a social virus, the cultural clutter known as *affluenza*. In their book *Affluenza*, authors John de Graaf, David Wann, and Thomas Naylor define the condition as follows:

> **affluenza**, n. a painful, contagious, socially transmitted condition of overload, debt, anxiety, and waste resulting from the dogged pursuit of more.

During the months that I worked with Gwen, she did indeed lose everything — or should I say, everything left her. That big SUV finally got taken away — replaced by an old, beat-up car, which was all she could afford. The condo and the house were gone. She lost her independence and moved in with a friend. Her wardrobe shrank down to the essentials. She even lost custody of her child for a time. And yet, as distraught as Gwen was with each of these life changes, her experience had a silver lining.

For the first time in her life, Gwen was forced to examine her belief system and the affluenza that put her in debt and turned her life upside down. Looking within was akin to taking a potent mindfulness vaccine. To her surprise, Gwen discovered she was dragging various kinds of damaging mental clutter with her every day. There was the fear that she couldn't succeed on her own and that she wasn't smart enough or strong enough. Then there was the emotional clutter from her family and culture that told her that she had to be independent and that it was wrong and shameful to ask others for help.

To recover, Gwen learned to acknowledge and understand how the more-bug and other daily beliefs had infected her. In their place she told a story she hadn't expected — one filled with profound clarity and a deep recognition of what was really important and fulfilling in her life. No longer being chained to this emotional (and physical) clutter, she forged a new life, one based on values and strengths that nourished her and those around her.

Gwen not only made an effort to connect with others in a meaningful way, but she willingly accepted help from others and let go of her limiting stories. She started recognizing and appreciating her ordinary daily strengths. You could say that she remade herself from the ground up — one new story at a time. Eventually, she got a small home of her own, a job she could feel good about, and importantly, regained shared custody of her child. I was grateful to have worked with Gwen — someone who put in tremendous effort in order to move her life in a whole new direction.

MINDFUL APPRECIATION OF THIS ORDINARY MOMENT

One of the reasons why newness is so exhilarating, exciting, and enticing is that the pleasure centers in our brains get a positive jolt when we experience novelty. However, once we become habituated or acclimated to a new thing and its novelty wears off, we again need something new to give the same good feeling we originally felt. In this way, we get stuck on what psychologists call the *hedonic treadmill* of wanting more pleasure. If we're wired this way, is there any antidote to always wanting more? Are we doomed to remain on the treadmill?

In Buddhism, there is a wonderful metaphor that depicts this insatiable craving for more. It is called the hungry ghost, which is often illustrated as having a tiny mouth, a long skinny neck, and a huge belly. In other words, the hungry ghost has a gigantic appetite that can never be satiated. It can never fill up that huge belly of desire because it has such a tiny mouth and neck. Living as a hungry ghost goes beyond material hunger; this is the emotional hunger and fear that drive envy, jealousy, greed, and all forms of possessiveness. Read the news, and you can see that even people with countless millions often need more — even if it means harming others. Without question, experiencing life as a hungry ghost produces a lot of suffering in the world.

Surprisingly, you need not look far to find the healing remedy for the hedonic treadmill and the hungry ghost. It's right here, right by your side, and it comes from appreciating this seemingly very ordinary moment. What if we could counter the desire for more by getting more satisfaction out of what we already have in our lives? Mother Teresa eloquently spoke of this in her poem "True Drops of Love":

> Do not think that love, in order to be genuine,
>   has to be extraordinary.
> What we need is to love without getting tired.
>
> How does a lamp burn?
> Through the continuous input of small drops of oil.
> If the drops of oil run out, the light of the lamp will cease,
> and the bridegroom will say, "I do not know you."
>   (Matthew 25:12)
>
> My daughters, what are these drops of oil in our lamps?
> They are the small things of daily life:

faithfulness,
punctuality,
small words of kindness,
a thought for others,
our way of being silent,
of looking, of speaking,
and of acting.

These are the true drops of love.
Be faithful in small things because it is in them
    that your strength lies.

Mother Teresa knew the deep truth of which she spoke. A study published in *Psychological Science* titled "A 'Present' for the Future: The Unexpected Value of Rediscovery" investigated the importance of ordinary experiences. Basically, researchers wanted to know what people would find more fascinating to review at some point in the future: an ordinary experience or an extraordinary one? At the beginning of the study, participants predicted that the ordinary would not be very interesting for them to review in the future. Then, individuals actually chronicled both an ordinary day and an extraordinary day through taking photos and writing about the day. The extraordinary day was Valentine's Day, and the subjects (all of whom had romantic relationships) wrote down their experiences of this special event. Three months later, subjects rediscovered their earlier experiences — the ordinary and extraordinary — to determine which they were more curious about and which was more satisfying. So which was more meaningful and curiosity provoking? Subjects found that the ordinary day's events were more meaningful and of interest than that special Valentine's Day. They had greatly underestimated that ordinary day and what they could gain from it. This study reveals the surprising power of the ordinary.

The ordinary contains the seeds of meaning and daily appreciation that dissolve the need for accumulation. Appreciation of the ordinary is a different way of being in the world than feeling acquisitiveness or envy. You're not likely to be envious of what another person has if you are deeply appreciative of what you already have in your life. By witnessing the incredible wealth and richness of ordinary and good things all around, you conquer feelings of scarcity, comparison with others, and appetite for more.

A wonderful example of how to savor the ordinary came from a friend of mine who commented on how fast her children were growing up. It made her sad, she said, to think that she might forget any of it. She responded by engaging the ordinary in a way that was at once simple, beautiful, and profound.

"Early this morning," she told me, "I sat in the shadows in a room just off the kitchen and watched my sixteen-year-old go into the kitchen to make his breakfast. He didn't know I was watching, but I just sat there as he broke an egg on the frying pan. He shook the shell. He adjusted his earbuds and then broke another egg. Just watching him moment to moment was my meditation. It was ordinary and very special."

Even the ancient Greek Stoic philosophers recognized that contentment came from appreciating the ordinary. Essentially, they would ask themselves the question, What would life be like if I didn't have those simple things that make my life tolerable and good? By imagining the loss of the ordinary, they came to appreciate it even more. No wonder that the ordinary is your secret weapon against the daily glut and clutter of affluenza.

LIFESTYLE TOOL: Appreciating and Savoring the Ordinary

For this practice, you will pay attention to the "small things," as Mother Teresa referred to them. When this becomes a daily practice, you will be surprised by how much you have that brings joy.

Find a quiet place where you can sit and reflect for at least five minutes without being interrupted. Read through the four categories below for appreciating the ordinary. Contemplate on these, or write down your thoughts. If you find that one or two of these methods resonate with you, bring them into your life each day as an antidote to daily clutter.

1. Savor Small Things That Bring Joy

Think about the small things that you cherish or just appreciate — they could even be daily rituals that bring order to your day. Here are a few examples:

- A cup of hot coffee in the morning
- Reading the paper
- Giving a hug or kiss to someone special
- Greeting a coworker with a smile
- Watching your child crack an egg
- Feeling your feet touch the floor in the morning
- Noticing the water while in the shower
- Appreciating the color of the walls in your home or office
- Sunlight
- The flavor of the first bite of food in the morning
- A comfortable chair to sit in
- The transportation that helps you get around

2. Observe Ordinary Things Right Next to You

Look around the environment that surrounds you. What ordinary things could you appreciate or savor that are nearby?

Throughout your day, get in the habit of taking a mental picture of the ordinary thing you are doing at that moment — from sitting down in your office to driving the kids to school. Let yourself steep in the beauty of the ordinary. Remind yourself that this moment is special and will never be repeated in the same way again.

3. Soak in a Past Success

In the same way that you can appreciate an ordinary moment that is occurring right now, you can also look back to appreciate a past moment where you felt proud and happy.

Right now, think of an accomplishment that made you proud — whether graduating from school, helping another succeed, getting a promotion, committing to self-care, or recovering from an illness or difficult time in your life. Spend a good five minutes letting yourself feel good about this event.

4. Remember a Past Kindness

Was there a time when you helped someone? Or when someone helped you? Of course, there was!

Right now, bring to mind that moment or event when you shared a word of encouragement with another, or vice versa. Remember, even the smallest and most ordinary act of kindness — a smile, a pat on the back, a word of encouragement — is a powerful expression of caring that can have long-lasting effects.

How can you bring ordinary kindness into the world today? Make a commitment to kindness, and write down your kindness or share it with others so that you don't forget.

∞

Chapter 13

PUT THE BRAKES ON WORK AND SPEED

I feel the need...the need for speed!

— Maverick and Goose, *Top Gun*

There's no question that we are feeling the need for speed in our modern culture and world. Speed makes all kinds of things more convenient (or so we're told). We can get almost anything shipped right to our door within a day or two. We are promised pizzas in less than thirty minutes. We receive instantaneous long-distance responses from others via texting and other forms of communication. Activities that took hours — like going to the bank and shopping in a store — can be done remotely by pressing a few buttons on a mobile device or computer. Even purchasing items in person can be done without a time-consuming cash transaction, shaving off a few more seconds of "wasted" time. It's all good, right?

There's nothing innately wrong with getting things done

faster. But if we're saving so much time through all these conveniences, why do we feel so stressed-out? Why do we seem to be running faster and faster throughout the day? Why do we seem to have so little time to reflect or just take a breath? That's because we're doing more with all that "extra" time. We try to cram two lifetimes of experiences into one. We try to have a satisfying job, be an engaged parent, entertain our friends, enjoy exciting hobbies, read our favorite books, eat at that tasty new restaurant, do a fantastic workout practice, and throw a great party like Martha Stewart. As a result, our lives often feel like they are splitting at the seams. There are only so many transitions we can handle in a day, and handle well.

The irony is that the more we try to do and the more transitions we navigate, the less time we have for deeper exploration. We multitask at work and are actually less productive. Our busy lives leave little time for long, meaningful, uninterrupted face-to-face time with family and friends. With limited time to cultivate our own hobbies, we watch from the sidelines to see how others fish, bike, hike, cook, travel, and participate in life. We read a few pages of a book here and there, but we don't have the time or mental concentration to quiet the mind enough to read for an hour or even thirty minutes. Instead of swimming in the deep mysteries of the ocean, we wade in the shallows of the pool.

In a recent workshop, I led the participants through a five-minute meditation. Afterward, more than one person commented on how nourishing it felt, but they also said they felt guilty about spending five minutes just being present. They felt as if they should have been doing something productive!

Speed and multiple transitions are forms of daily clutter that keep us running and feeling like we can't quite catch up to life's ever-quickening pace. Speed changes our expectations by feeding our impulse for instant gratification. I call this the *Las Vegas*

Nerve, the 24/7, get-it-now-or-feel-unhappy nerve. Speed also adds to the number of daily transitions that we have to make — which can leave us feeling exhausted if we don't learn how to manage transitions. Combine speed with the fact that technology makes working at all hours of the day and night easy to do, and you have a potent daily clutter combo. That's the equivalent of supersizing your emotional clutter.

One man who played a role in how we live and work today was Frederick Taylor, who in 1911 wrote *The Principles of Scientific Management*. Taylor brought the stopwatch into the workplace in order to increase efficiency and labor productivity. Initially, people resisted the idea of working more like machines, and his ideas were met with riots and even a congressional investigation. Over a hundred years later, Taylor's ideas have become embedded in the American psyche and workplace. Even in the healthcare and medical fields, the amount of time spent with patients is shrinking. The increase in productivity is creating greater physician burnout. We have become faster and more productive, but at what cost?

To better understand the effects of fast-paced living, social psychologist Robert Levine decided to measure the pace of life in large cities around the world. How does urban life affect health? His research, published in the *Journal of Cross-Cultural Psychology*, examined the speed of life in thirty-one different countries. The study used two ways to gauge speed for each location. First, researchers timed how long it took people to walk a city block during rush hour. They also timed how long it took postal workers to complete a particular task.

Levine's work showed vast differences in speed for societies around the world. Japan took the honors as the fastest country, along with several Western European countries. Generally speaking, the pace of life was fastest in economically developed areas, cities that were colder, and places the researchers termed "individualistic cultures." The real shocker was that faster cities had significantly higher rates of death from heart disease and increased levels of smoking. Those living in faster places were also found to be not as willing to help or lend a hand to strangers. If you live in one of these type-A cities, what are your options?

✦

One young man who was a casualty of speed and efficiency was Alan, a twenty-five-year-old warehouse worker who was making a good salary. His job was to drive a forklift and move large pallets to the shipping dock. He liked his boss, and he had been promoted more than once. The only problem was speed. Alan's workflow and activities in the warehouse were closely monitored by a GPS device, which he wore around his neck. Whenever he picked up a new pallet, the device would start timing him. Each trip from the warehouse to the dock was timed and recorded. Eventually, Alan cracked under the pressure. He couldn't sleep; he worried that he wasn't being fast or efficient enough and that he'd lose his edge. Before long, he started having panic attacks at work, until finally he couldn't function. He took a week off work, which seemed to help, but his symptoms quickly returned.

When he initially came to see me, he just wanted to be "fixed." After some questioning, I learned that Alan was not the only one at his workplace who was struggling because of the demands for greater speed and productivity. Others had been unable to cope with the pressure and ended up leaving. Although we worked to reduce his anxiety, Alan eventually came to realize that this job was not a good fit. Could he have forced himself to adapt to this pressure of being more machinelike? Probably. Would it have been healthy, satisfying, and sustainable for him in the long run? Probably not.

SLOW THE PACE WITH MINDFUL TRANSITIONING

Here's what you need to know about transitions: they tend to increase one's level of stress and anxiety. They do so because, when we transition, we are uncertain about what will happen next. It's not that transitions themselves are negative; it's *how* we make the transition that matters. When we can make transitions consciously, with full awareness, we may not feel the same level of worry and anxiety. There's also a large social component to transitioning. For example, each time you leave your home in the morning, you are making a major transition from your home base. Whenever we leave, it helps to get closure of some kind as well as to maintain a sense of connection. How did you leave your home this morning? Did you hug your partner and others in the household? Did you mention that you will stay in touch during the day?

When working with couples, I like to ask about one small change they would like their partner to make that would improve the relationship. I emphasize that the change should be small, realistic, and achievable. More often than not, the requested change centers around a simple, daily transition of going and coming. One woman wanted her partner to give her a goodnight kiss before going to sleep. One man wanted his spouse to get out of bed in the morning, give him a hug, and tell him "Have a nice day" before he walked out the door for work.

Similarly, any time that we enter a setting — such as our home, workplace, or doctor's office — it's important that we feel secure and included. A man I worked with said he wanted his partner to stop watching TV when he came home so that she could greet him and talk with him for five minutes. Then there was the woman who felt very unsettled when going to work because nobody greeted her. Everyone had their heads buried in their computers. We came up with a plan that had her connect with one person she knew well. This one change helped her feel safe and that she was part of the team.

There are many different kinds of transitions. A transition occurs when we physically move from one place to another. Transitions happen when we switch from one task to another, such as from writing an email to planning a grocery list. As already mentioned, transitions are social and occur when we depart or return from the people in our life. Transitions can be emotional as well; they can be caused by a change in how safe we feel. An argument with a work colleague or romantic partner, for example, can transition us from calm to upset in a heartbeat. All of these transitions can be difficult. Which of these different types of transitions create the most clutter for you? How do you respond to these various transitional clutter moments?

Here are four basic ways to manage transitions.

1. **Reduce the overall number of transitions in a day.** By cutting down on your transitions, you naturally reduce the amount of uncertainty and anxiety you encounter. This is a form of simplifying your life. Suppose, for example, your to-do list for the day includes exercising, going to the doctor, grocery shopping, clothes shopping, finding a gift for your friend's wedding, making dinner plans for the weekend, and picking up the kids from school. Instead of cramming all of this into a single day, you can lessen the clutter by lumping together two or three activities that are in physical proximity to one another, and creating another grouping that could be done the next day. By reducing the number of transitions you make in a day, you lessen anxiety and tap into greater simplicity and a sense of calm and peace.

2. **Limit the number of different projects during each day.** Spend a substantial amount of time concentrating on

a single project instead of shifting back and forth between several. Research indicates this approach is more productive and keeps you more focused. Save your Facebooking and other social media for a short block of time rather than returning to it often. When you are doing an activity, be fully present with it. Be aware of when your attention wanders from the task at hand. With this strategy, you will accomplish more and feel less mentally exhausted and scattered.

3. **Pay attention to how you transition when leaving and entering.** When you or another is leaving, make sure you have a sense of closure and connection, either through touch, words, a gesture, or a smile. When you or another is entering, make certain you do what is necessary to feel welcome, safe, and secure, such as by making direct eye contact, getting up to greet that person, or getting off an electronic device. Create a ritual of your choosing — such as a handshake or a hug.

4. **Slow down and be present as you transition.** Don't rush through your transitions as if they were onerous chores. Treat even an ordinary event — like cleaning up after dinner — with a sense of curiosity or sacredness. In some spiritual traditions, the most mundane chores — like cleaning the toilets and scrubbing the floors — are saved for the most advanced students. That's because these students understand that each moment holds the seed and gift of presence — regardless of what activity you are doing. This sentiment is described in the well-known Zen phrase: chop wood, carry water.

If you're walking to get the mail, why rush? Can't you wait a moment longer to see all the junk mail and the bills? Step slowly to the mailbox. Feel your feet touching the ground, notice how miraculously your body moves. Feel your fingers on the mailbox. Let yourself experience how you pull down the handle and reach inside. Sense the textures of the different pieces of mail as you slowly move and balance the mail in your hand. Watch this entire mail dance with amazement, for no two trips to the mailbox are identical! Would you want to miss out on this just to get to the next thing, and then the next, like a robot?

Wise transitioning requires thoughtfulness, planning, effort, and discipline. If we go through the day without giving thought, thinking we are free to do as we choose, we may be missing out on the real freedom to transition with full awareness. Sufi master Inayat Khan and Buddhist monk Ajahn Amaro make this point in their own unique ways:

The path of freedom
Does not lead to the goal of freedom;
It is the path of discipline
Which leads to the goal of liberty.

— Inayat Khan,
The Gayan: Notes from the Unstruck Music

The mother doesn't simply let the child
do whatever the child wants to do;
some discipline needs to be established.

— Ajahn Amaro, *Finding the Missing Peace*

LIFESTYLE TOOL: Palm the Present Moment

This practice is a multipurpose, portable tool for managing transitions by countering anxiety. You can use this method anytime you need to slow down before or after a transition, or when you feel your mind is too busy and spinning too quickly and you want to get more present and in the moment.

Find a quiet place where you can practice this for at least five minutes to start. Once you are familiar with how to "palm the present moment," you can shorten the process and do this in just one minute, if desired.

✦

Sit in a comfortable chair, and take a couple of nice, long, calming breaths. Press your feet into the floor, and let yourself feel grounded and connected with the earth. You might even think of your favorite tree; picture yourself connected and rooted to the earth like that tree.

Now raise your hands up to the height of the heart center, with the palms facing one another — about a foot or so apart. Notice how much tension there is in just holding the arms and hands up in the air.

Next, ever so slowly, bring the hands closer until you feel even the slightest or subtlest sensation of energy, pressure, heat, or warmth between them. Stop when you feel this, and just notice this for a few moments. Observe this sensation closely. Is the heat, warmth, energy, or pressure constant? Or does it vary slightly moment to moment?

Now gently move the palms closer until just the fingertips come together with the most feathery, lightest touch. Imagine that the molecules from the fingertips of your right hand are dancing with the molecules of the fingertips of your left hand. You might even think about what dance they are doing — the fox-trot, the samba, the tango, the waltz, or the jitterbug.

Continue to bring your palms together until they lightly touch. As you do this, notice how the fingers straighten out and how more heat builds up between the palms. Notice even the subtle change in the positioning of the wrists.

With your palms together, pause for a few moments to appreciate your body, which is a precious gift that we all possess. For ten seconds or more, reflect on the wise words of former priest and author John O'Donohue, who wrote, "Your body is the only home in the universe."

Now spend a few moments tensing and relaxing the body. Keeping your palms touching, raise your elbows up to the side. Press with only 10 percent of the total pressure you could exert. Next, press your hands together even harder — up to 20 percent of total pressure. Stop pressing if you feel any pain. Press only as hard as you can without experiencing pain or discomfort.

Observe how far up your arm the tension goes. Does it extend to the wrists, the elbows, the shoulders, the shoulder blades, the back, the chest? Do you feel more heat building in the palms of your hands? Which muscles are tense? After about five seconds, let your shoulders and elbows relax and fall. Release all this tension. Notice how nice it is to let go of tightness and tension in the body.

Finally, very slowly open your palms, like flower blossoms opening to the morning sun. Sense the coolness in your palms as the heat dissipates. Let the weight of gravity tug on your hands and arms, letting these gently fall like leaves from a tree until they come to rest on your lap or legs.

Take a breath in — picturing that breath as a golden light coming in from the crown of the head or from the nose or mouth. Let that light fill up any part of the body where there is tightness, tension, or a negative emotion. As you exhale, picture this breath carrying out all of the tension, tightness, or negative emotion down the legs and out through the bottom of the feet back into the earth for recycling.

Take another nice, long inhale, and as you exhale, imagine any remaining stress draining out with the exhale down your legs and out of the bottom of your feet — where it will flow into the earth for recycling. If you wish, take an extra breath to remove any further tension.

If you want, just sit for a few more moments in appreciation of the body that follows your commands and carries your consciousness so you can achieve your life goals. How marvelous!

∞

Chapter 14

NATURE'S CLEANSING POWER OF HOPE

Negativity is totally unnatural. It is a psychic pollutant, and there is a deep link between the poisoning and destruction of nature and the vast negativity that has accumulated in the collective human psyche.
— Eckhart Tolle, *The Power of Now*

The clutter of daily cynicism and negativity is a true pollutant. More than ever, we need nature as a touchstone for hope and wisdom. Nature possesses the unique ability to sweep away the veneer of cynicism and tap the wellspring of hope that lies dormant. When I speak of hope, I think of this as something that is real, not hypothetical.

You may be familiar with the Greek myth of Pandora's box. Pandora is a nature goddess whose name, according to some, can be translated as the "all-giver." As the story goes, the all-giving nature goddess opened this box — the ultimate container of negative clutter ever assembled. It contained all the ills, evils, and suffering of humankind. In the broad mythical sense, this made

Pandora's box the holder of all that we cannot fathom; it is all the things we find impossible to deal with.

Pandora closed the box, but not fast enough to keep these plagues of clutter and confusion from escaping. This sounds like a very unfortunate story. What are we humans going to do with the terrifying and overwhelming contents of that box? All seemed to be lost until it was discovered that one small thing remained in Pandora's box. And that small yet powerful antidote was hope.

Looked at another way, it is only by setting free our clutter that we can connect with hope. So long as we cling to despair and negativity, hope is buried, unreachable, and unattainable at the bottom of our clutter pile! Fortunately, hope isn't such a small and powerless thing after all. The psychologist Erik Erikson once wrote, "Hope is both the earliest and the most indispensable virtue inherent in the state of being alive. If life is to be sustained, hope must remain, even where confidence is wounded, trust impaired."

The story of Pandora assures us that through the offerings of nature we can access the sublime, empowering, and transformative gift of hope. Through our deep connection with nature, we are witnesses to the mystery of life's cycles. We are not lost but comforted by nature's lessons. We grow to understand that discovery, destruction, despair, openness, hope, rebirth, and renewal follow one another as the morning dawn follows the darkest night.

Nature portends the path toward greater peace, wholeness, and freedom from the poisons that exist. If we do not respect nature, if we do not steward it and guard it, it will die. And with it, maybe, too, will the hope that sustains our best dreams.

Hope, of course, needs to be made real.

What is the real, down-to-earth purpose of hope? Henry David Thoreau said it well when he wrote, "To affect the quality of the day, that is the highest of arts." Hope is capable of doing this in so many wonderful and little ways. And yes, spreading hope is an art form because your expression of it is unique to who you are and to where and how you use it — whether in your profession, at home, or in everyday life.

The truth is, no broken school system, tribe, culture, or institution can change without hope. No broken adult, child, or family can heal without hope. No broken world can find peace without hope. And so, as a starting point, why not plant seeds of hope and optimism around you, in your life and your community?

You can plant the seed of hope with your patience and a kind word while waiting in a long line for your latte at Starbucks; you can plant it through each compassionate decision you make at your workplace; you can plant it by being patient and understanding with loved ones after a difficult day of tending to others; and you can plant it by consulting with colleagues when you need a wise solution to some difficult problem.

Hope takes many forms, and all of them reflect the fact that whether we like it or not, we are all floating in the same leaky boat (our city, state, and planet). We can't plug those holes alone. That is why hope also acknowledges that when one person suffers — from indignity, from poverty, from cruelty, from injustice, and from prejudice — all of us suffer.

So when you give hope to another, you ease suffering. With hope, you really *do* change the world one small, compassionate act of living kindness at a time. Whatever your calling may turn out to be, whatever the roles and responsibilities, one of your most important jobs is to serve up hope for those who have little or none.

The question remains, though, how do we access nature's and hope's cleansing power? How can we act as a rebellious band of Johnny Appleseeds, spreading and planting seeds of hope and positive change with each step we take and everywhere we go? It's easier than you may think.

✦

During my divorce, I experienced a dark period of despair and feelings of hopelessness. I always thought that divorce was something that happened to others; I never imagined it would happen to me. Still, my wife and I agreed to separate, and on Christmas Eve, she went to spend time with her sister in Atlanta. Meanwhile, I spent the following nights alone in the frigid house, feeling lost, like a ship without an anchor, adrift in the murky, choppy ocean.

It was early January, and my house was literally frigid because I was trying to avoid spending three hundred to four hundred dollars a month to heat the house. I had a cord of wood that I burned sparingly, along with wearing a thick wool sweater and a ski cap indoors. As I huddled close to the fireplace, my wife and I sent several heartrending emails back and forth. We both exuded a sorrowful, fearful, and desperate tone, and I was left feeling deeply disheartened. I wanted to find a solution, but it seemed as impenetrable and frustrating to me as a Rubik's Cube, a puzzle I could never solve.

Not sure what to do, I walked to the back of the house and looked outside. The sky was clear and smooth as a crystal vase. As I had done so often in difficult times past, I sought out the peace, beauty, and solace of nature. And so I stepped outside, feeling the chill air on my face and hands. Then, pulling the ski cap snugly over my ears, I walked up the grassy yard a ways and sat down on a small bench that faced the tall fir and cedar trees. I lifted my gaze upward to the gently swaying treetops and expansive, starry sky. What I did next may surprise you. It did me.

I let my worries go.

You read that right. I released it all, gave it up to the trees, the sky, the infinitely greater and wiser hand of nature (the Divine, the Mystery, God, or whatever name you prefer). It was akin to simply opening a cage and letting a captured bird fly free. My eyes moistened, and I just kept letting it go — the not knowing, the uncertainty, the pain, the heartache, the longing for a solution, the fear, the sadness, the doubt, the wishing it was different. I gave up my worries in this way without expectation as tears rolled down my face.

It's hard to describe what happened next. As I sat there, I lost track of time. The individual self — "Donald," the one who was convinced this was all happening to him and who strongly identified with it all — went into abeyance, into hiding. Don't ask where he went. Maybe he just got a little smaller, a little less important, because with "Donald" cut down in size, there was no longer the sensation of the cold bench or the frozen ground. There was just this expansiveness, this space, this sense of connectedness. There was no longer this separate individual who was looking at the sky and trees. Somehow, "Donald" got absorbed into the big picture, into the great cathedral of trees and the black mystery of space and stars.

It didn't come to me in words, though I have since put words to it:

It's all the blessing.

It's *all* the blessing. The good, the bad, the divorce, the fears, the monetary settlement, all of it, however it turned out. Yes, all of it was the blessing. Although I had wanted to find a solution, something concrete and fixed to remedy my problems, I had instead been graced with a *soul-ution* — an unexpected, heart-filled path that gave me the much-needed hope that I could move forward and that all would be well.

I don't know how long I lost my "self" in the big picture. I only know that at some point I was immersed in a vast and deep ocean of peace and contentment.

Suddenly, as if shot out of a cannon, I felt myself return to my body and the backyard. My feet were numb, in pain. My hands were stiff and prickly from the cold (and from foolishly not putting on gloves). Shivering, I stood and quickly went back inside the house, where I crammed as many logs as would fit into the fireplace and started a nice, warming fire.

Later that night, I sent a short email to my wife, telling her about my experience. While I hoped at the time that it helped her, it sure helped "Donald" — and whoever else was in there — to know that there was more at work here than my own limited thoughts and self-interest.

In case you're wondering, the expansive feeling that I got that night didn't stay with me. During the divorce process I continued to experience fear, anger, and all kinds of upset. But when I did, I reminded myself that nature had spoken to me of how *it's all the blessing* — even if I didn't think so in the moment.

Years later, nature continues to transport me to a wise and healing place where the logical and rational mind couldn't possibly venture. How you will connect with nature is hard to say. Maybe you'll go for a long walk by the ocean, forest, or other sacred spot. Maybe you love the mountains. You don't have to be especially religious or spiritual to let nature send you its healing and clutter-removing power of wisdom, light, and hope.

ACCESSING NATURE'S POWERS

A field of study known as Attention Restoration Theory was shepherded by psychologist Stephen Kaplan beginning in the 1970s. This work has helped explain the immersive and engaging power of nature, which Kaplan termed "involuntary attention."

Voluntary attention, on the other hand, is what you use when you make decisions, study, work on a business plan, make a shopping list, or even cross a busy street. While voluntary attention takes mental energy and can leave you feeling exhausted (think how you feel after working on a project for several hours), involuntary attention restores your mental energy. It refreshes your mind, so to speak, and more.

Research has shown that taking time to view nature offers many benefits. For example, just a few minutes spent in nature can restore our ability to think and concentrate. Looking at nature has been shown to help people in hospitals heal faster. Nature has been shown to reduce stress, aggression, anger, and even mild depression.

A study published in the journal *Computers in Human Behavior* investigated how spending time in nature could help preteens recover their lost ability to recognize nonverbal emotional cues. A group of fifty-one preteen students were tested for their ability to notice facial and emotional cues. These skills were shown to be limited, and the students made a lot of errors in naming emotions. The students were then taken to an overnight nature camp, where they had all their mobile devices and screens taken away. For five days, the students engaged in face-to-face interactions. After just five days of nature and personal exposure, this group significantly improved their abilities to recognize and correctly name emotional cues upon being retested. This seems to indicate that nature can reverse the effects of many kinds of physical and emotional clutter.

Sometimes, nature can provide a burst of insight when nothing else will work. Wendy, a sixty-four-year-old client of mine, shared a story of hopelessness. "Every morning I go to work, go inside my office, shut the door, and cry," she told me, her voice trembling. "Everyone is being laid off. I've lost most of my friends, and I know my time is coming soon." To make matters worse, Wendy's adult daughter had lost her job and house and was moving back home. For Wendy, it meant retirement was not going to be possible.

I worked with Wendy using tried-and-true cognitive behavioral therapy. It helped somewhat, but her fear and worries resurfaced. One day, Wendy came into my office with a different expression. She had a look of resolve and determination, along with a sense of peace and calm. I asked her what had happened that changed her demeanor.

"I went outside during my morning break and sat on a small bench in the business park courtyard," she said. "I was sitting there, looking at this tree from the top of the branches and then down toward the ground, when I noticed something I'd never seen before. There were some invasive vines that a gardener had snipped away. But the vines had started to grow again." Her voice brightened as she leaned forward. "I saw them and it hit me: I'm like those vines. It's in my nature to keep going, not to quit. The vines didn't stop growing just because a gardener cut them back. Neither will I. It's who I am!"

Soon after, although Wendy lost her job as she had expected, she was undaunted. Her insight from nature gave her what she needed to continue her journey — which she did by finding another job in what must have been record time.

The ideas below are ways for you to tap this source of hope throughout your day. I think of nature as vitamin N.

LIFESTYLE TOOL: Inviting Nature

Here are two different ways to get your daily dose of vitamin N. Get creative as you contact nature, and you'll soon find that you're making connections several times a day, even if it's just for a few seconds here and there. These moments of presence with nature are restorative and potent ways of transcending the world of thoughts and resting in the here and now. Find patience as you invite nature, for as it is said in the Tao Te Ching, "The softest waters carve even the hardest stones."

A Five-Second Nature Meditation

For the duration of one nice inhalation and exhalation, place your gaze at nature's doorstep. Breathe in the natural surroundings, drawing them into your body and mind, letting them settle into your cellular being at all levels. Exhale out any tension, tightness, or negativity that exists in the body or mind, letting them drain out the bottom of your feet and back into the earth.

Notice any of the following for your Five-Second Nature Meditation:

A tree
A plant
A bird, animal, or pet
The sky
The ground
A leaf
A branch
A cloud
The empty air
Water (in a river, lake, cup, faucet, or fountain)
Your body moving as you breathe
Another person
A piece of paper (and the clouds, trees, and nutrients that
   made it)
A pencil (and the trees, water, and minerals that made it)
A cup of coffee, tea, or other beverage

Sky Gazing Meditation

The Sky Gazing Meditation is a way of connecting your gaze with nature. It begins by extending the gaze toward the sky or horizon and then slowly bringing it downward to focus on a nearby tree or plant.

This short, easy-to-use practice can be done indoors or outdoors in a matter of minutes. Use it anytime you feel the clutter of mental fatigue or being overwhelmed. This meditation will help you get centered and refreshed, quieting your busy mind. After you are done, you will likely feel more refreshed and ready to focus and concentrate.

While you can adapt this practice indoors by using any size plant, the ideal is to be outside with a tree and a view of the sky or horizon. Follow these five steps for approximately five minutes:

1. First, go outside and find a location that ideally includes a view of a large tree and the sky above or beyond — so that you can easily transition your gaze from the sky to the tree while standing in place. If you can, stand within arm's length of this tree. If that is not possible, stand close enough to see the details of its bark and leaves. Try to choose a tree that is pleasing to you and draws you in — perhaps because of the color of the leaves or the shape of the branches or the trunk.

2. To begin, slowly raise your head and cast your gaze out as far as you can into the sky. Visualize releasing or letting go of whatever troubles and worries you have into the expansiveness above you. Let go of the uncertainty, the not-knowing, the fear, the sadness, the doubt, and even the wishing it were different. Release all of that into the sky, which is infinitely spacious and big enough to hold all the worries of the world. Stand as long as you need to, continuing to let go and let be.

3. Place your hands on the tree as you shift your gaze from the sky down to where you connect with the tree. Imagine that your feet are rooted solidly into the earth like the tree. Did you know that trees are among the largest organisms on earth? Feel your connection with the great cathedral of trees that protect our ecosystem and make our lives possible. As you feel the bark on your hands and fingers, let yourself get absorbed into the big picture of how we are surrounded and sustained by the natural world.

4. Now, starting at the bottom of the tree, slowly turn your gaze upward. Pay attention to the smallest details, from the texture of the bark and changes in coloration to where new growth occurs. Continue to broaden your focus until your gaze reaches the highest branches at the top of the tree.

5. Rest the weary mind as you sense your unity with nature and the wisdom it holds. Appreciate the lessons of the natural world and of the seasons, how there is a time for planting, growing, harvesting, and pausing. Allow yourself to open to these teachings in the moments and days ahead.

When you finish, reflect on what it was like to spend five minutes with nature in this way. When might you find this practice most helpful? What was it like to release and cast your worries into the expansiveness of the sky? How did this help you separate from clutter and gain a different perspective?

∞

Chapter 15

DAILY FLEXIBILITY, SOFTENING, AND LETTING BE

Use the Teflon side of your mind, not just the Velcro side.
— Lama Surya Das, *Words of Wisdom*

Much of our pain comes from the clutter of resisting or hardening ourselves against the way things are. For example, how often do you resist what appears before you during an average day? Suppose you're stuck at a stoplight and late for work. Do you get anxious or frustrated and blame the red light and drivers for conspiring to make you late? Imagine you're in the line at the grocery store and someone pulls out a whopping stack of coupons at the last second. Do you lose patience, roll your eyes, and curse your fate — or maybe curse the coupon shopper? Or perhaps you observe a lackadaisical coworker who doesn't care or works only half as hard as you do. Do clutter feelings of anger and resentment stick to you like Velcro? Do you resist the fact that you have debts to pay? Do you resist that you don't have the career or life that you dream of? Do you blindly respond to new situations in old ways, rather than get playful and flexible?

Reacting to difficult daily events, whether minor or major, can be a challenge. That is, until we learn how to soften. It's not that life is conspiring to annoy and thwart us. Rather, when we mindlessly want reality to conform to our own limited mindsets, fixed categories, blind routines, rigid contexts, mental shortcuts, and narrow perspectives, this is what causes unwarranted and often inexhaustible mounds of needless clutter to pile up. Softening means that you can bend and not break; it means having an attitude of openness, willingness, and acceptance toward what life throws at you. The more pliable you are, the more you are able to change course and roll with life's punches — instead of throwing punches.

In the broader sense, softening ourselves is about nonattachment and letting go of toxic clinging, whether to a rigid political viewpoint or to some outward goal or reward. This is quite different from having wholesome desires and aspirations, which are inspiring and beneficial. But it's possible to get ensnared in the sticky web of attachment — and the resulting stress and unhappiness — even with healthy desires.

The trick is not to cling to even those wholesome desires or experiences, but to let go of expectations and to let each experience flow past you like a breeze. Even the person committed to being mindful will be miserable if he or she gets too attached to the idea of being present at all times! While it might seem like a paradox, nonclinging and letting go of the outcome actually open your heart and mind. They allow you to flow naturally, like a river that flows to the ocean without effort or worry.

TRANSFORM VELCRO THINKING
INTO TEFLON THINKING

My good friend and book author Randy Fitzgerald once shared with me his family's story about what it meant to be a "man." This coming-of-age ritual, handed down from great-grandfather to grandfather to father to son, illustrates how Velcro thinking — being stuck in a robot-like mindset — can pass through the generations. Here's Randy's story:

> At the age of eight, I was given a rifle and taken hunting with my father and a group of other men. My goal upon arriving at a big ranch in central Texas was to kill my first large animal. I had been told stories of how my father, grandfather, and other men in my lineage had successfully done this as young men.
>
> It was daybreak when I was left alone at a deer stand and told to wait for a buck to kill. The idea was for me to mount its horns to the front of the vehicle and return home in triumph. After a short time, I saw a family of deer — a buck, a doe, and a couple of fawns approaching. The buck was beautiful, big, strong, and graceful. I watched and waited in silence for them to come close as they grazed on grass and foliage. With the animal in range, I slowly raised my rifle and trained my sight on the buck that would be my prize, as well as gain me praise from my father and the other men.
>
> But I couldn't pull the trigger. I couldn't bring myself to kill this buck in front of his deer family. I knew I'd feel guilt if I killed this deer; on the other hand, I knew I'd be shamed and ridiculed by my father in front of the other men if I told them the truth about not killing it. I had never before lied to my father, but when he asked

me if I'd seen a deer, I said "no." I never agreed to go deer
hunting again.

While following generational mindsets or rituals without
questioning them may give us a sense of belonging, there are
times when Velcro thinking may actually affect our health and
how we feel and think about ourselves. I recall visiting an art gal-
lery where all the artists had an identified mental illness, such as
depression, bipolar disorder, and so on. Each artist wrote a touching personal biography, describing their illness and how important this illness was to their creative process. While the personal
stories were compelling and the artwork stunning and beautiful,
I could not help but wonder how identifying oneself so strongly
with a mental illness — or any fixed idea — might affect that
person's future growth.

Fixed ideas about aging are another example of how easily we
can get stuck in anxiety-ridden clutter — individually and cultur-
ally. In her book *Mindfulness*, social psychologist and mindfulness
researcher Ellen Langer described various studies about aging
that she conducted — studies that explored the psychological and
physical effects of switching from negative Velcro thinking about
age to more flexible Teflon thinking. Could a more Teflon-like
perspective about age bring our bodies to a more youthful state?
To find out, Langer recruited men who were between seventy-
five and eighty years old. The men were placed into one of two
groups. The experimental group attempted to re-create and act
like the person they were twenty years earlier, when they were
fifty-five years of age. The second group — the control group —
merely thought about the past as it had been twenty years prior.

To help the experimental group embrace the context of when
they were fifty-five years old, the men were brought to a rural
retreat center for five days. Everything in the retreat center — the
TV programs, advertisements, radio programs, magazines, and

music — was just as it had been twenty years earlier. The men were encouraged to talk about this context as being the present moment rather than thinking of it as the past. This group watched films from that year and had discussions about them. They also were encouraged to do things for themselves — such as taking care of their own luggage — just as they had done when they were fifty-five years old.

A visual recording was taken of subjects in both groups. This tracked posture, movement, and gait both at the beginning of the study and at the end, as well as a number of physical measurements. Independent judges even looked at before-and-after pictures of their faces to rate the ages of the men in the study.

There were significant changes between the two groups after only five days. The judges rated the experimental group as looking an average of three years younger after just one week. Other physical changes for the experimental group (as compared to the control group) included better hearing, increased flexibility and manual dexterity, greater finger length, improved eyesight, and even improved height while sitting. The experimental group also showed significant improvements in an intelligence test that was given to both groups. In *Mindfulness*, Langer concluded, "The regular and 'irreversible' cycles of aging that we witness in the later stages of human life may be a *product* of certain assumptions about how one is supposed to grow old. If we didn't feel compelled to carry out these limiting mindsets, we might have a greater chance of replacing years of decline with years of growth and purpose." These stunning findings suggest the importance of being more flexible in how we think about ourselves.

Even stubbornness can be a form of Velcro thinking. No one is immune to this, and I'll never forget the period in my life when I became "fixed" on being a screenwriter while living in Los Angeles. At the time, I believed that single-mindedness was a necessary requisite for success — and I soldiered on despite little advancement. Of course, sometimes sticking with a goal is useful and helpful, but sometimes our stubbornness can hinder us and keep us from exploring other possibilities. When I let go of that rigid thinking pattern, I was free to move into Teflon thinking and take my life in uncharted directions, for which I am grateful. Mainly, I learned a lesson about holding on too tightly. Not only is it all right to let go and change course — sometimes it is crucial to our growth.

Einstein used mental "what if" exercises to help him think about relativity in fresh, new ways, and we can teach our minds to be more flexible and Teflon-like using similar exercises. As a mental Teflon experiment, look around your environment and choose an object to focus on — such as a desk lamp, computer, TV, cell phone, book, chair, table, desk, and so on. As an example, let's use a desk lamp. You know the lamp's intended function — to provide light — but that lamp could be used for other things. Take the Teflon perspective and consider what those other functions might be by completing the following sentence:

A desk lamp *could be* _____.

By adopting a Teflon mindset, a desk lamp *could be* a lot of things — a paperweight, a hand warmer, a hand dryer, an exercise barbell, a doorstop, and a hat, if you removed the shade. Now, pick another object in the room, and consider how many other things that item *could be*. Again, I'm not saying you would actually use an object in all these ways. The purpose of this "what if" exercise is simply to get you thinking more flexibly, in a Teflon state of mind.

This same Teflon thinking could also be extended to the attitude you take toward any situation. Think of how you automatically respond to a daily challenge, such as morning rush hour. How many ways can you finish the following sentence?

My attitude toward rush hour *could be* _____.

From the Teflon perspective, your attitude toward rush hour could be many things — acceptance, fascination, amusement, self-compassion, compassion for others, willingness, and gratitude for having a place to go to during rush hour.

Now consider some other *could be* scenarios.

- My attitude toward my marriage/my relationship/my children *could be* _____.
- My attitude toward my job *could be* _____.
- My attitude toward anxiety *could be* _____.
- My attitude toward my need for control *could be* _____.

Sometimes, there's an unconscious or unintended benefit to our Velcro thinking. For one thing, we know exactly what to expect. There's also the emotional charge that comes from feeling righteous and angry about situations that are out of our control — and yet this gives us a false sense of power and mastery. When impossible things happen in the world and in our lives, it may feel like it's easier to ignore or rail against the truth of life's messiness than to accept it. In the long term, though, this just produces a suffocating wall of clutter.

DAILY AFFIRMATIONS FOR BREAKING FREE FROM VELCRO THINKING

A study published in the journal *Proceedings of the National Academy of Sciences* examined how negative or positive thinking affects immune system function. More specifically, the researchers wanted to measure whether those individuals who had high levels of activity in the left prefrontal cortex — which is associated with optimism and positive emotions — would display a greater immune system response when given a flu vaccination.

Fifty-two subjects were given several emotional memory

tasks. By looking at the responses and the prefrontal cortex activity, researchers pinpointed individuals who tended to react pessimistically and those who reacted in a positive or optimistic way. Next, all subjects were given a flu vaccine and were examined three times over a six-month period. This was done to record how many antibodies were in the blood — a measurement of the body's immune response. The results clearly showed that people who had a more positive emotional style had a stronger immune response than did individuals who were negative. Richard Davidson, one of the study's researchers, concluded, "Emotions play an important role in modulating bodily systems that influence our health."

Constant dwelling on negative clutter, or Velcro thinking, creates a well-worn groove in the brain that plays over and over just like a favorite song — one that we now know affects the body's health. Affirmations provide us with a means of blocking old negative songs while giving us a new and more positive tune to align with. A new mental soundtrack, created through a conscious affirmation, holds the potential to transform both our emotional and immune response. At the same time, we need to catch those mind whispers — the very subtle and almost unconscious commands — that can sway us and cause us to act robotically.

As you think about using conscious affirmations, it's important to feel any resistance you may have to them. Bringing any resistance into the light will help defuse it. It will also help you to understand just how deep and unyielding old clutter can be. In *Scientific Healing Affirmations*, spiritual teacher Paramahansa Yogananda recognized that potent, positive affirmations could be weakened or immobilized by background clutter. He wrote, "If you affirm 'I am well,' but think in the background of your mind that it is not true, the effect is the same as if you took a helpful medicine and at the same time swallowed a drug that counter-acted the effects of that medicine."

The Lifestyle Tool below shows how a carefully chosen and caring affirmation can buffer you from negative clutter zones. As you rewire your brain in this way, you will sweep away rigidity while simultaneously inviting greater flexibility and receptivity into your life.

LIFESTYLE TOOL: Affirming the Positive

Here are a number of affirmations that you can try. Some come from different traditions and can be used like mantras — sacred phrases that are repeated over and over. Others are simply ways of reminding ourselves of what we want and how we want to be in the world.

1. Affirmations of Personal Strengths and Qualities

- I am safe.
- I am intelligent.
- I am caring.
- I am calm.
- I am patient.
- I am a woman/man of great love and beauty.
- I am open and accepting.
- I am flexible and spontaneous.
- I am adventurous.
- I am peaceful.
- I am positive.
- I am inspiring, energizing, and activating.
- I am _____.

2. Affirmations for Centering, Calm, and Acceptance

• Don't sweat the small stuff.
• Don't take it personally.
• Not too fast, not too slow, get in the flow.
• Everything will get done.
• All you need is love.
• Give peace a chance.
• It is what it is.
• Just be me.
• I deserve the time and space to heal.
• Good enough is good enough.

3. Affirmations for Spiritual Connection and Support

• Lord Jesus Christ, have mercy upon me. [This ancient Christian prayer is sometimes called the Prayer of the Heart; said silently throughout the day, it expresses faithfulness to the Divine and your values.]
• *Om mani padme hum.* [This Tibetan mantra translates as "The jewel of awakening is in the lotus"; it is a reminder to be mindful and to awaken our consciousness.]
• *Om tare tuttare ture soha.* [This ancient mantra of Tara, the feminine and compassionate aspect of the Buddha, translates as "Blessings to Tara, the one who saves others"; this mantra invokes the compassionate Tara energy to support our endeavors.]
• *Om gum ganapatayei namaha.* [This ancient Hindu prayer of Ganesha translates as "Salutations to Ganapati, or Ganesha, the remover of obstacles."]

Which of these affirmations resonate with you?

There's no right or wrong way to use affirmations. You can write down your favorites on an index card and keep it with you.

Or you can store favorites in your phone for reference throughout the day.

These affirmations just scratch the surface. There are spiritual affirmations in all traditions for almost anything, from happiness to prosperity. You can also adapt any of the sayings above so that they feel right for you.

As with any of this book's Lifestyle Tools, it helps to make a habit of using affirmations. Notice how your thinking — and behavior — responds as you keep your affirmation firmly in mind.

∞

—— *Part 4* ——

Transformation
and Fulfillment with
Peace, Purpose,
and Wholeness

Removing ancient and daily clutter is a worthwhile path that paves the way for a whole life. But a whole life depends on deepening our wisdom and learning how to stay receptive and open in order to bring the gift of purpose into the world. Living in service with others enhances and sustains. Most importantly, it cultivates co-healing and furthers the heart-filled path toward peace and fulfillment for all.

Chapter 16

AWAKEN THE COMPASSIONATE HEART TODAY

The best and most beautiful things in the world cannot be seen nor even touched, but just felt in the heart.

— Helen Keller, *The Story of My Life*

It's easy to erect a wall around the heart. After all, who among us hasn't experienced hurt, trauma, or addiction in some form or another? If you have a human body — and I assume you have brought yours along as you read this — then you know the truth of loss, sadness, grief, and various kinds of emotional and physical pain. These forms of suffering can be viewed as a "bad" thing, but they can also be an opportunity to open the heart and to recognize that suffering is a universal human condition that we all share. This recognition serves as the pathway through which we can cultivate a more awakened, trusting, and compassionate heart.

As precious and temporary as life is, how can we not risk opening even the wounded heart?

If we lock ourselves in the jail cell of hurt, loss, and unfor-giveness, we do ourselves a disservice. To close off the heart is akin to what songwriter Joni Mitchell described when she sang, "They paved paradise and put up a parking lot." Paving over the heart in an effort to shield it from hurt only produces a barren, cold place. Fortunately, a blade of grass always seems ready to burst through the tiniest crack in the concrete. Such is the ever-lasting persistence of the heart's renewal.

Our brains have evolved to love and bond with others. Love is as natural an impulse as taking a breath. In *Just One Thing*, neu-ropsychologist Rick Hanson wrote, "The brain has tripled in size since hominids began making stone tools about 2.5 million years ago, and much of this new neural real estate is devoted to love and related capabilities. We need to love to be healthy and whole. If you bottle up your love, you bottle up your whole being. Love is like water: it needs to flow." If our flow of love has stopped be-cause of self-centeredness, mistrust, disappointment, injustice, or a host of other causes, how can we get it moving again?

✦

Jenny was a high school senior, just seventeen years of age, when she came to see me for debilitating migraines, depression, and anger. She was very mature despite the many arrows of sorrow that pierced her. Jenny had never met her biological father, and because her mother struggled with various forms of addiction, Jenny was sent to live with her aunt and uncle at the tender age of seven. Though her mother was no longer a substance user, she seemed incapable of loving her daughter — something Jenny wanted more than anything else in the world. Jenny's mother was very narcissistic and was more interested in her own life than her daughter's many accomplishments at school.

Each visit with her mother left Jenny feeling unwanted,

unappreciated, and depressed. Forgiving past hurts and injustices is something many adults are unwilling to undertake, so I was unsure whether Jenny would jump on board. But in our talks, the idea of forgiving her mother resonated with Jenny. We discussed why forgiving helps us lessen our own pain — not by forgetting what another has done, and certainly not in ways that allow further abuse. As a homework assignment, I asked Jenny to find some meaningful quotations about forgiveness. One quote that resonated with her was by Mahatma Gandhi, who said, "The weak can never forgive. Forgiveness is the attribute of the strong."

Jenny was able to do something very special — she gave up her expectation that her mother should apologize for her misdeeds and act differently. Instead, Jenny focused on making space in her heart for her mother's own struggles and suffering.

It wasn't easy. Jenny meditated on loving-kindness before and after seeing her mother in order to keep her heart open and heal each fresh wound so that her pain and anger wouldn't fester. Jenny also learned that by forgiving, she was offering a very special gift to her mother, something that no one else could give her. I was proud of Jenny's effort to remain compassionate toward her mother, which remains an ongoing life lesson in softening and opening her heart.

I am reminded of the story of one of the Dalai Lama's monks who was tortured for years while in a Tibetan prison. After his release, he was asked what was the most difficult challenge he faced during his incarceration. He answered that it was the time he began to lose compassion for the one who was torturing him. That the monk did not pave over his heart to make a parking lot is a testament to the heart's resilience and its ability to overcome hatred and fear.

These stories, and others like them, tell us that keeping the heart open is a process. The heart may suffer unspeakable hurts, but it contains the multiple antidotes of love, hope, forgiveness, resilience, and compassion.

TUNE IN AND TURN ON TO COMPASSION

Have you ever felt the natural impulse to help someone in need without thinking about what's in it for you? This is compassion — a kind of helping that doesn't come from a place of ego gratification or self-centeredness. Compassion is more encompassing than altruism or charity. It's also broader than the feeling of empathy that comes from putting yourself in the shoes of another. In addition, compassion is not about thinking, "Look how good a person I am for helping others." If anything, a compassionate perspective encourages us to broaden our view and consider the larger social good.

Scientists have begun studying compassion by exploring how the practice of loving-kindness — an ancient meditation for directing feelings of love and caring to oneself and others — affects such things as negative thinking, depression, and even pain. A study published in the *Journal of Personality and Social Psychology* investigated the effects of the loving-kindness meditation on working adults. The researchers found significant differences between the control group and those who practiced the meditation. They concluded, "This meditation practice produced increases over time in daily experiences of positive emotions, which, in turn, produced increases in a wide range of personal resources (e.g., increased mindfulness, purpose in life, social support, decreased illness symptoms). In turn, these increments in personal resources predicted increased life satisfaction and reduced depressive symptoms."

In another study, a team of researchers at the Duke University Medical Center demonstrated direct effects on the body from loving-kindness meditations using forty-three adults with chronic lower back pain. The mean age of participants was 51.1 years, and each had experienced chronic pain for at least six months. The intervention involved eight weekly, ninety-minute loving-kindness group meditation sessions. Compared to the control group, those practicing loving-kindness significantly reduced their levels of pain, anger, and psychological distress. Post and follow-up analyses also showed significant improvements, while no changes were recorded in the usual-care control group.

At a fundamental level, compassion transforms our brains. Scientists have conducted studies in which monks who have practiced over ten thousand hours of compassion meditation were put into MRIs to evaluate their brain function. The results revealed that the monks' compassion-trained brains featured high-amplitude, synchronous gamma waves — an unusual brain wave pattern that is believed to be the signature of a highly functioning brain.

Fortunately, it doesn't require five years of intensive practice to get the benefits of compassion. Compassionate action grows simply from understanding the universality of suffering and its roots. You begin by noticing that people's actions are often motivated by either wanting pleasure or avoiding pain. We need only examine our own life experience with the Eight Worldly Winds (see chapter 4, page 49) to understand how grasping for what is desirable and pushing away what is undesirable produce the clutter of suffering.

When you penetrate the truth of this, you clearly see ignorance, avarice, delusion, or hatred without needing to respond in kind. Sweeping these harmful emotions away, you are free to respond with love, understanding, and compassion.

Consider the following questions for bringing a compassionate heart to others:

- If I asked my heart for advice about a difficult predicament I currently face, what insight, wisdom, or deeper truth would it offer?
- If my heart could express how it feels about wanting to heal an important relationship in my life, what would it say?

Of course, the best place to start applying compassion is at home. Instead of interpreting our sorrows as pathology — calling them depression, anxiety, and the like — we can see their source: the stickiness of clinging and unhealthy attachments that keep us stuck. Getting stuck in this way is the nature of life itself. Why blame, shame, or call ourselves names?

We can sit with the knowledge of our own sticky human nature — a very healing way to greet this moment. Accepting the conditions that have produced our anger, our sadness, our anxiety, and our depression dramatically shifts our personal identity. Each time we send compassion to ourselves, we pull out suffering at the roots. It's a slow, but honest, decent, and hospitable way to treat ourselves. Of course, you are always welcome to label yourself as defective and in need of repair, but then remember: How does that make you feel? Has that mindset ever helped you solve anything?

It is better to practice self-compassion. Here is an easy way to begin. Take a few moments to try the following:

- Begin by thinking of some action, word, or thought that hurt someone else — and that you blame yourself for.
- Think of some action, word, or thought that caused harm to yourself — either intentionally or unintentionally.
- Knowing that no one is perfect, how can you bring greater self-acceptance and self-compassion into your life? Can you choose to open your heart and soften your view of those hurts?

Since all of us have done something to hurt ourselves or someone else at some point, spend the next minute forgiving yourself for an action, thought, or deed that caused harm. Even if you don't believe that you deserve this forgiveness, offer this as a gift to yourself, and see how it feels.

✦

It was a warm, sunny afternoon in Southern California when I was invited to join some friends who were having lunch with a spiritual teacher, whom I had heard of but never met. When it was time to say good-bye, I prepared to shake hands with the spiritual teacher. Instead, he wrapped a big, warm bear hug around me, and I reciprocated. Instantly, I felt something subtle, something unusual, which I could not put into words.

As I turned to leave the room, it happened. A tingling as sweet as honey spilled warmly down my back and neck, soon covering my entire body. All my cells felt as if they had been immersed in the energy of pure love, as if an inner light had been switched on. As this giddy sensation filled me, I could not suppress the wide smile that spread across my face. By the time I stepped outside, I was so engulfed with an overwhelming sense of joy and well-being that I had no idea where I had parked my car!

By nature, I am a skeptic. Maybe that is from being raised by an engineer father who approached everything with a scientist's mindset: if something wasn't observable and couldn't be explained, then it wasn't real. But here I was, powerfully and undeniably immersed in the energy of loving-kindness — a meditation that I had long been practicing and had learned from other teachers.

All my previous loving-kindness meditations had served as preparation, and now I knew what it felt like. More importantly, I knew with absolute certainty that it was real, as real and powerful as the juice in an electrical outlet. And it could be transmitted by anyone willing to practice it, just as the Buddha had taught more than 2,500 years ago. Despite having had several mystical experiences throughout my life, this one finally helped me break the irrational hold of my rational mind.

LIFESTYLE TOOLS: Awakening the Heart with Loving-Kindness

Find a quiet place where you can sit, stand, or lie down as you do this meditation, which consists of movement, visualization, and words.

Begin by setting the intention to open, awaken, and soften your heart. This is a nondiscriminating kind of love that you extend to yourself and all beings — friends, neutral people, and even unfriendly people — as well as to those you love and care about. Don't try too hard — just let your heart and being naturally do the rest. Use this anytime that you feel fearful or when your heart is closed and walled off.

Loving-Kindness Meditation

Begin by slowly cupping your hands and palms, one at a time, over your heart. Hold that position softly. Let yourself feel the warmth between the hands and your heart. If you don't feel warmth, imagine a golden glow, and bask your heart and hands in that warm glow. If your heart feels heavy, or as if it has a wall around it, give that wall permission to lessen and dissolve.

Let your heart's own protective wisdom glow and grow warm. Take a nice, long in-breath, breathing in the love of the universe — as well as the love from all the benefactors and spiritual people who have graced your life or whom you admire. Imagine this love as a golden light that illuminates your heart, softening it and making it glow with warmth and kind feelings toward yourself and others.

Now, slowly move both hands outward from the heart. As you do this, extend the heart's warmth and glow so it stays connected with your palms. Continue to breathe in the love of your benefactors and of the loving universe into your heart. Move your hands outward until they form a semicircle in front of you. Your arms are open and receptive and connected to your heart energy. Imagine this glowing warmth of the heart spilling outward, overflowing toward others. You might picture this as a bubble that extends outward, with the bubble enveloping everything it touches inside its golden, glowing sphere. This glow creates inviting warmth, a warmth of availability to others. It is also protective, keeping you safe while extending the nondiscriminating wish for the well-being of all others.

Finally, if you'd like, picture the golden glow of loving-kindness expanding and extending far, far beyond you, into the neighborhood, the county, the state, the country, the hemisphere, the world, the solar system, the universe, and all universes and all beings. Hold this glowing light for all suffering ones.

To conclude, bring your hands back toward your heart center. Again cupping your palms over your heart, send loving-kindness to yourself. Say or think the following words:

> May I be safe, happy, healthy, and well. May I be free
> from pain, hunger, and suffering.
> May all beings be safe, happy, healthy, and well. May all
> beings be free from pain, hunger, and suffering.
> May I be available to act on behalf of those who suffer.

Last, take a nice long breath or two to reorient yourself to your surroundings and the present moment. As you exhale, slowly allow your hands to fall at your sides, ending your practice.

During the day, you can do this entire practice or any of the individual parts — just the movement, the visualization, or the words. Here are two examples for centering with loving-kindness that take less than a minute:

1. Mentally say the following words throughout the day as a way to stay centered and keep your heart open: "May I, and all beings, be safe, happy, healthy, and well."

2. Whenever you feel hurt, angry, or closed, simply cup your hands over the heart center as you connect with your heart's warm, compassionate glow. Breathe in compassion and forgiveness, and breathe out the hurt. Take from one to three breaths in this way.

Also, you may want to ask yourself the following questions:

- When can I integrate this practice into my day?
- How can I put compassion into action and be available to others?
- How can I journal my experiences and invite others to try loving-kindness?

∞

Chapter 17

FIDELITY TO THE MOMENT

To be truly alive is to feel one's ultimate existence within one's daily existence.

— Christian Wiman, *My Bright Abyss*

S aint Benedict was a sixth-century Italian monk whose Rule of Saint Benedict laid out guidelines for those on a spiritual path. To that end, novice monks were instructed to take a vow of *conversatio morum*, which translates as "fidelity to monastic life." But the word *conversatio* means a "conversion of life," and in this sense it holds a deeper meaning. In their book *Contentment*, authors Robert Johnson and Jerry Ruhl consider this to mean "a vow of fidelity to the moment...designed to help support men and women who were embarking on a spiritual journey." One way that Benedictine monks practiced fidelity to the moment was by singing and reciting prayers seven times a day. Anyone can use the wonderful concept of fidelity to the moment as a modern means of clearing out clutter.

Fidelity to the moment can dramatically transform how we experience something that is normally taken for granted. Such was the case for my friend Benny — a former drug addict and now a compassionate addictions counselor — on the first day of his sobriety. On the day Benny made the commitment to live a sober life, he found himself walking down the street in New York when he smelled something sweet, something alluring in the air.

Benny had no idea what it was, but being curious, he followed the scent around a corner. To his delight and surprise, his nose led him to a beautiful, flush red rose bush. He was stunned by the flower's beauty. That rose became a symbol of his waking up from the trancelike grip of addiction and cemented his fidelity to the moment. With fidelity to the moment, you contact that rose, that person, that morsel in a direct and fresh way — instead of just having the mind label it as "oh, there's another rose," or "oh, there's Joe again."

It is in this same spirit of fidelity to the moment that Robin Williams's character exhorts his students in the film *Dead Poets Society*: "*Carpe diem*. Seize the day, boys. Make your lives extraordinary."

SIMPLIFY, SIMPLIFY, SIMPLIFY

Real estate agents always emphasize "location, location, location" as being one of the most important factors when buying a property. Likewise, simplifying one's life is a factor that can help us to de-clutter our minds and surroundings in order to live each day with greater fidelity to the moment.

The idea of simplifying is, well, simple. You have less to worry about, fewer things to fret over, and fewer choices to make. I'm not recommending that you trade in your car for a horse and buggy (good luck finding that horse-and-buggy dealership), but you can differentiate between "more than enough" and "enough." Making this distinction can act as a guide for how to simplify and downsize, as well as whether you need to upsize or upgrade.

As a former technology junkie, I now upgrade software or devices only when my computer freezes up or will no longer operate. Yes, I have occasional pangs of screen envy when I see people holding supersized smartphones. When this happens, I remind myself to revalue my phone — which I do by remembering how nicely it fits in my pocket and does everything I need it to do. Revaluing and appreciating what you already have is a good way to embrace simplicity and counter the urge for "more than enough." Simplicity breeds peace of mind and removes the worry over always trying to get the newest and latest.

Differentiating "enough" from "more than enough" can be applied to your surroundings — both home and office. In my own kitchen, for example, I once had a cabinet crammed with more plastic containers than I would ever use. I cleaned them out and donated most of them, leaving me with "enough." Now I can open the doors without having three or four containers spilling out onto the floor. I've also addressed excess clothes in the closet and boxes that have remained unopened in my garage. I decided what to clean out on the basis of the question, If I haven't opened this box or used this article of clothing in the past year, why is it still here? This question applies to physical clutter, but it embodies the mindset for keeping things simpler and streamlined.

Simplifying your life pertains not just to things but to how you use and manage your time. Time is a precious resource, and using it wisely is important for your emotional well-being and balance. If you're cramming too much into a day, a week, or a weekend, notice how that makes you feel.

Research shows that adopting a simpler lifestyle may pay positive emotional dividends. Psychologist, researcher, and writer

Robert Biswas-Diener has traveled the globe trying to under-stand how simplicity plays a role in emotional satisfaction. To learn more, he spent months investigating Amish communities that emphasize simplicity. Of his research findings, he wrote, "The Amish are faring pretty well, psychologically speaking. I... found that they had high average life satisfaction. When it came to emotions, 100% of the respondents were above the neutral point."

Simplicity, of course, is not just about how many things we need, but how many activities are sufficient. If your social calen-dar is booked solid and you feel exhausted just thinking about having to do so many activities, it's time to simplify. This may mean setting boundaries — limiting how late you'll work or play with others. You have the right to set boundaries for self-care, and this is a type of simplifying that can give you more fidelity to the moment — rather than being stressed-out and not savoring the moment because your schedule is too complicated and over-whelming.

The following Lifestyle Tool gives you several methods for awakening to the moment. Fidelity to the moment is not just a practice but a way of being. The more you apply fidelity to the moment, the more you will access it with ease and a new appreci-ation for the sublime ordinary.

LIFESTYLE TOOL: Fidelity to the Moment

To embrace fidelity to the moment is to enter into each moment without holding on to expectations or preconceived ideas of how this moment is supposed to look or be. Zen masters think of this as "don't know" mind. How wonderful it is to not know all the an-swers. How nice to not be saddled with the pressure of being right or wrong. To risk the moment means to reclaim the same childlike awareness that you once had naturally. There is no success or failure here, just fidelity to each fresh moment as it unfolds.

1. Fidelity with the Breath

When you lose fidelity to the moment, you can always reconnect by taking a long, slow breath. Ask yourself: Is this breath yesterday? Is it tomorrow? With a single breath you regain fidelity to the moment. Breath is the essence of nonattachment; try to hold on to any breath too long and you'll faint.

2. Fidelity with Another

Soften up and receive another person with your presence. Let go of your prejudices about this person and how you would like him or her to behave and act. Even if you believe this individual to be the most difficult person in your life, open to who is really there. Get curious. Open your eyes, your ears, your senses, and all the pores of your body. Hear beyond the words; listen with the dimensions of emotion and empathy. Don't just look, but *see* into the person's eyes, face, and being.

Speak volumes with your love and acceptance. Whenever you notice the tendency to put another in a mental box, to label people or move them around like chess pieces or objects, step back, breathe, and soften again. Imagine each person as a movable tree on two feet. Notice and appreciate each tree with amazement, for there is no other like it in the entire universe.

3. Fidelity with Yourself

Empty your cup to receive. Let go of who you *think* you are. Let go of all the stifling conditions that tell you what you're supposed to do and how you're supposed to act. You spend a lot of time pretending you're somebody. Why not pretend you're nobody so you can let in some air and light and space?

4. Fidelity with the Sense Body

The body is a cornucopia of now. You only need to tune in and listen to its sense-sational symphony of vitality, feelings, and aliveness. Notice when you are in your head and out of your body. At that moment, notice your feet on the floor. Let yourself get grounded like a favorite plant or tree by pressing your feet into the floor or earth. Bring your consciousness into the whole body from the tips of the toes to the top of the head.

Wherever you feel negative clutter, tightness, tenseness, or any stress, breathe into that part of the body. Imagine your breath filling up the tense area. Then exhale, letting your breath carry away any negative emotions or body tightness down the legs and out through the feet where they are deposited in the earth for recycling. Take as many of these cleansing breaths as needed.

If there are feelings in the body — sadness, grief, loss, anxiety, depression, frustration, loneliness — take them seriously as the body's wisdom telling you that something in your life needs to change. Honor these feelings while knowing that they do not define you as a person. Try to name the emotion for the physical sensation that your body is sending you. That will help you to understand it more. Finally, take action — such as getting support or help — in order to find more harmony within.

Rest in this precious gift. Settle in. Now, bask the entire body in the glow of gratitude for all that it does for you on a daily basis. How wonderful!

5. Fidelity with Walking

Soften and become flexible when walking. Move like a cat. Notice all the body's movements, the lifting of each foot, how each leg swings forward, how each foot lowers and presses into the ground, the suppleness of the ankles, and how the body shifts its weight from one side to the other.

Above all, when walking, just walk. There's nothing else to do, really. So long as your body is pointed in the right direction, you won't get lost. Dare yourself to bump into something, but it's almost impossible when you have fidelity to walking. Walk to be *here*, not to get *there*.

6. Fidelity by Stepping Back and Simplifying

When you feel overwhelmed by stress or any situation that fills you with clutter, observe yourself as if from a distance. Imagine you are on a hilltop or in a helicopter viewing what was happening. From this safe vantage point you don't have to take things personally. You can be present without being reactive. If a situation can be eased through simplifying, then allow yourself to simplify. With this more Teflon-like viewpoint, reflect on what options are possible, so that you can skillfully respond in the moment. Even evoking an attitude of self-acceptance or self-compassion for yourself during a difficult time is a skillful means of having fidelity to the moment.

✦

These Lifestyle Tools are like putting cleanser in the tub: they only clean when you do some scrubbing.

Try all the above practices; get in the habit of using them. After a time, these practices will be naturally integrated in your day, and you'll find fidelity to the moment comes easily.

To begin, try scheduling these Lifestyle Tools by putting them into your to-do list or appointment book. See which ones work best for you. Put together your own unique combination of tools for enhancing presence, Teflon mind, and daily softening.

∞

Chapter 18

BECOME A MASTER AT UNTYING KNOTS EACH MOMENT

If you want to untie a knot, you must first find out how the knot was tied.
For he who knows that origin of things knows also their dissolution.

— Buddha

Have you ever met or known anyone who didn't have some troublesome, negative baggage that they dragged along behind them? Imagine that emotional baggage as a big ball of beautiful silk fabric bundled up in knots. Each knot signifies an emotional entanglement, an unhealthy addiction, or a habitual reaction of anxiety, jealousy, anger, or frustration. The softness of the fabric and its free-flowing design are no longer easily felt or seen because of the tightness of the knots that have accumulated over a lifetime. This bundle gets so tight that sometimes even the knots have knots. What does your ball of knots look like? How big is it, how heavy? How difficult is it to pull behind you each day? Most importantly, what would it be like if you could untie these knots — and even untangle the fabric before new knots form — so your ball of clutter became less cumbersome and more manageable?

Believe it or not, you can untie even the most unyielding and unwieldy knots in your life. What would this look like? Imagine someone who has an open, accepting attitude toward life's ups and downs. Someone who seems free of entanglements like jealousy, greed, and envy — a live-and-let-live individual who doesn't get consumed by negativity from the past or by anxieties about the future. Certainly, such people feel disappointment, impatience, and frustration, but they know how to let them go — without tying an extra knot around that situation. As Zen master Bernie Glassman said in *The Dude and the Zen Master*:

> When stuff comes up and at a certain point it feels like it's too much, move on. It's not going anywhere and there'll be a time when you'll be ready to work with it. For now, listen to yourself. If it's not the time, don't push it. Gently down the stream. Some people say you have to work with everything, but there's a time and a place. If it feels like a knot, wait. It will come up again when you and the universe are ready.

There's wisdom and self-kindness that comes from not having to "fix" or resolve a knotty situation. Instead, you can take a breather, knowing that giving yourself space and time isn't a cop-out so long as you consciously step back. Don't worry; the knot will return, and you will have an opportunity to work on it again.

THE KNOT-RELEASING POWER OF PAUSING, NAMING, ACCEPTING, AND RELEASING

Suppose it's your weekend off. Your children are staying with friends, and you actually have space to relax for the first time in ages. But then, on Saturday evening, just before going out with friends, you are contacted by your workplace to deal with scheduling issues. You do that, and then you awake Sunday morning and it happens again. Right before you are going out the door for a cherished cup of coffee and a yoga class, you are interrupted and forced to deal with more work issues.

You decide to email your friend Bonnie about your experience regarding this potentially knot-tying work interruption during your cherished weekend off. Here are two very different emails — one that draws the knot tighter, and one that loosens and untangles it:

To: Bonnie
Subject: Tying the Knot

Outside yoga center for 10:30 yoga class. Barely made it here, no thanks to work. Can you believe it — work calls and texts on Sunday morning!? I am really angry. It's so unfair that they keep pulling me out of my day off. They have no right. I'm not looking forward to going into the office tomorrow.

To top it off, I had to prep the kids' dinner in crockpot. Had to change menu at last minute, but was so upset I couldn't think of what to make. So. I don't even feel like doing yoga. Guess I'll try.

To: Bonnie
Subject: Untying the Knot

Outside yoga center for 10:30 yoga class. I need it. Got up to prep the kids' dinner in crockpot. Had to change menu at last minute. Work calls and texts. I found myself slightly irritated. Why did they pull me out of my day off again?

I wondered and let it go.
So. Grateful to be here.

The first email shows how easily one can get entangled with negative emotions. The second email takes a different approach entirely. While you might think the person writing this second account is just taking a let-it-go attitude, the writer is approaching this very skillfully. This second email actually utilizes a four-step process of (1) pausing, (2) observing and naming emotions, (3) accepting the emotions and situation as temporary, and (4) releasing them and letting them be. This is a process that has been scientifically shown to help untie emotional knots in the moment. Let's explore this process in more detail.

A study published in the journal *Appetite* investigated food cravings in overweight and obese individuals. The researchers wanted to know if mindful awareness and acceptance of cravings would break the maladaptive cycle of binge eating and food craving by helping individuals mentally disengage from the cravings. Subjects in the study used a seven-week training that focused on observing and developing acceptance of food cravings. At the end of the study, these individuals had significantly lower food cravings.

Researchers concluded that the possible reasons for this included "disengagement of obsessive thinking and reduction of automatic relations between urge and reaction." What this means is that participants were able to pause and step back. Rather than fuse with their cravings — so that they felt no separation from the craving and identified themselves with it — they were able to *observe* and *name* the craving as if from a distance. This stance of stepping back let them *accept* the craving and notice it moment by moment, instead of just *automatically reacting* to it and giving in to it. The process of pausing and naming the craving (or emotion) helps us disengage from it. This has the effect of interrupting and stopping the old, automatic reactive or addictive behaviors from occurring. In this way, mindful awareness and attention actually serves as a brake between an urge and the automatic response to act upon it.

Instead of trying to suppress an urge or resist it, acceptance is more effective because it demonstrates how any craving or emotion is temporary. It will eventually subside and fade away. That's a powerful thing to know, and that's why acceptance unties those sticky knots, even the old ones, right here and now. The same process of disengaging from cravings or negative emotions applies not only to food cravings but to other toxic behaviors and addictions — from hard addictions, such as to drugs, to so-called soft addictions like internet sex and pornography.

Now, let's deconstruct the messages hidden in the two emails. Reread the first email, and notice how there is no separation from the negative emotions. With the phrases "I am really angry" and "so upset I couldn't think," the sender of this note is pulling the emotional knot tighter. The person is, in effect, saying "I am" this emotion. In fact, the negative knot is tightened several times and even projected into the future: "I'm not looking forward to going into the office tomorrow." Long after the actual event is past — spending a few minutes to resolve the work issue — this individual is still carrying past clutter while entering yoga class. There is no further thought, inner reflection, or inquiry about what has happened. And there is definitely no releasing of the knot.

Now reread the second email and notice the subtle distinction between noticing the emotion and fusing with it. Here, the sender disengages from the emotion with the words "*I found* myself slightly irritated." The person skillfully pauses to observe and name the emotion and even the level of irritation. The person also reflects inwardly by asking, "Why did they pull me out of my day off again?" This is important because it is the act of questioning that helps us to disengage. The moment you question something, you are making the event, craving, or emotion the object of your attention. Now, you are thinking about the knots and reflecting on them rather than creating new ones.

Finally, the sender reaches a place of acceptance and release, writing, "I wondered and let it go. So. Grateful to be here." By finding gratitude for being at the yoga class, the person lets go of what happened and returns his or her attention fully to the present moment. The person is no longer carrying a heavy and unwieldy bundle of knots while practicing yoga poses.

SHINE THE LASER LIGHT OF INQUIRY TO LET GO AND GET IN THE FLOW

As human beings, we're all subjected to different forms of emotional knots of clutter that latch on to us — so let's explore how to let them go and get in the flow as you go through your day. First, it helps to accept that there is going to be clutter. You will, at some point, find that knots have been created. But your attitude in the face of them can make a difference. The key is to not be so focused on the ever-blowing winds of the external world.

Instead, bring more focus to the presence of your inner world. A heightened inner awareness — along with the Teflon-thinking skills from chapter 15 — will help you soften and stay open and adaptable even in the face of new clutter. Let's look at how to shine the inner light of inquiry at the mind itself — as a way to stay present, centered, and free of new knots.

Imagine you are in a traffic jam and late for work, a meeting, soccer practice, or something else. To make it worse, someone cuts you off, nearly causing you to crash, and then makes an unkind gesture toward you. Maybe you lose your temper and shout or raise your fist, or even dangerously tailgate the offender. This is an example of how things that happen in a split second can cause you to have a powerful, negative reaction. Negative events often happen so quickly that we don't have time to slow things down and think about how to respond, rather than immediately react.

Let's practice slowing things down. Picture in your mind's eye a similar, but actual, event that caused you to react in a similarly upsetting and habitual way as in the above example. Call to mind a real button-pushing scenario. Put yourself back into the situation, and feel your negative emotions and what they do to your body. Pause to take a long breath or two. Now shine the high-powered laser light of inquiry inward by asking the following questions as you continue to breathe:

- Where did this knot first get formed? What's the knot's origin?
- What are these emotions I'm feeling from this knot?
- How strong are they?
- Who do I know who exhibits a similar reaction?
- How did the knot get so strong?
- How many times have I reacted like this in my life?
- Am I just a robot acting out?

Now, really, *really* turn the laser beam on high as your inquire further about your knot. Don't think too hard. Let it flow.

Picture the knot. Now, imagine your own wise, inner lama suddenly clapping his or her hands together and jolting you with the questions, Who?! What?! Where?! Ask yourself:

- What feeling am I avoiding or craving in this situation?
- Why am I not accepting what is happening right now?

You may not have all the answers, and may never have them all, and that's okay. What's vital is inquiring, asking, and breaking an old pattern of responding automatically. Congratulations on having the courage to pause and shine the light of inquiry to look within.

As you were inquiring, were you still upset, angry, frustrated, or impatient — or feeling whatever emotion you originally experienced? Likely not, and that's because you shifted your perspective in a very fundamental and profound way. You became a neutral observer instead of being held hostage by an old, conditioned robotic response.

After inquiring, let yourself become more expansive. Let the knots loosen just a little bit more. Notice how you feel by loosening your grip and not holding on too tightly. That knotty situation in your life may remain, but you don't have to tighten the knot. In fact, you can loosen it by being present with what is happening whenever you get exposed to it — just by inquiring and being open to your experience. Then allow yourself to release it by being fully present in the here and now. That knot is not permanent after all. Untangle one, and they all begin to loosen.

LIFESTYLE TOOL: Untying Knots Using a "Pebble"

Here is a useful Lifestyle Tool for remaining present and not getting entangled in knots. Do this meditation for up to ten minutes a day, or anytime you feel that knots are tightening around you. Find a quiet place where you can sit undisturbed. The purpose of this meditation is to quiet your mind. The meditation employs the metaphor of a pebble resting below the surface of the turbulent waters of the mind. The pebble settles at the bottom of the ocean or a riverbed, where the water (the mind) is still and serene. By placing attention on the pebble, your mind gently turns away from all those wild and untamed thoughts. In this way, the pebble meditation teaches the weary mind how to rest.

The Pebble Meditation

Picture a pebble resting on the ocean floor or a riverbed. It might be perfectly round or have smoothed-out ridges. Imagine it in your mind's eye, seeing how its colors and shape glisten and sparkle as the sun's rays shine on it. Visualize the clear, still waters around your pebble.

Your pebble has no agenda. It is just being a pebble, with a pebble's-eye view of all the fish and fauna that surround it. But the pebble remains still, stable, safe, and secure, no matter how many knots and thoughts swirl near the surface of the water. Observe from the pebble's perspective how the knots loosen and are carried away with the water's swift currents.

If you want, imagine what it would be like to be the pebble. Know that there's nothing for a pebble to do, but to simply "be." And breathe. There is just this pebble inhaling. Just this pebble exhaling. If you notice an attractive fish (a pleasant thought) swimming past, you can follow it, then return your attention to your pebble breath and body. If there's a knotty fish or even a shark (a persistent negative or scary thought) that won't go away, you can always open your eyes and do the Pebble Meditation another time. Usually, though, that scary fish will swim away after a time, and you can return to your pebble breath and body.

If it helps, you can also choose a pebble "word" to focus your mind. Choose a word or phrase that is neutral or comforting — such as *one, peace, calmly resting, pebble, green,* or another word that doesn't stimulate your mind or create a lot of mental associations. Don't force the word. Just favor this pebble word over other thoughts — while remaining aware of your breath and body. If your mind wanders or follows a pretty fish thought, that's okay. Just gently return to your pebble word or phrase.

✦

How does this practice settle your mind? Are you able to stay with your pebble breath and body — and the pebble word, if you have one?

As with any de-cluttering practice, this one works best when used regularly. Consider scheduling this practice. What times of day would be most effective or helpful to loosen daily knots?

∞

Chapter 19

TAKE DAILY SNAPSHOTS OF JOY

Be content with what you have, rejoice in the way things are. When you realize there is nothing lacking, the whole world belongs to you.

— Lao Tzu

Here's some wonderful advice for being miserable: *Ignore all the good and decent things that surround you in the course of an ordinary day.* Here's more: *Complain about the things you can't change, and even complain about those things you can change.* The list could go on — because we've all been there. I'll never forget a talk I gave for my book *Living Kindness* at a bookstore in the local mall. We had a nice, intimate audience of about twenty-five interested people.

I decided to open the talk with a question to get the pulse of the group. I asked them, "How many of you have felt grateful for something in your life already today?" It was just a tad past noon, so I figured everyone had enough time to notice *something* they could appreciate. Running water. The sun. Warm clothes. Being

healthy enough to stand and walk. The availability of food —
just steps away at the mall's food court. The comfortable and stable chairs they were sitting on. Not a single hand went up. They
weren't being contrary — they just hadn't noticed the ordinary,
decent, good things that were right next to them.

It's an easy trap to get into. With all the high expectations
and levels of stimulation we experience, the only thing that seems
to catch our attention is the newest and latest glittering object or
dramatic news. It doesn't help that we are wired to notice novelty, as well as being seduced into believing we can buy happiness
through retail therapy. I don't blame anyone for this. This is the
fishbowl that we're swimming in. But if you really want to do a
mind sweep of daily clutter and feel appreciation for what you
have, there's no better — nor less expensive — way than through
locating joy. Or go to a soup kitchen or talk with those who are
poor. Sometimes, to appreciate what we have, we simply need to
wake up and look around.

Let me make a couple of other points about joy and why it is
sometimes ignored or misunderstood. First, to steep yourself in
joy does not mean you are trying escape from the reality of life's
difficulties or hassles. Just because life contains challenges or loss
doesn't mean that you can't also — even simultaneously — shift
your awareness and experience joy. This is the beautiful ambiguity
of life. It is not a simple equation, like $1 + 1 = 2$. Joy and suffering
coexist, just as light contains all the colors of the rainbow. To be
fully alive, we need to find the joy that is hidden in plain sight,
right beside us.

Second, joy is not a guilty pleasure, something that means
you are not being productive. After all, joy is not really productive, is it? And that's the point. Joy actually counters the mech-
anistic view of life — that we measure ourselves by how much
we produce and do, like a machine. Joy integrates the seemingly

disparate parts of our life. With joy, it's the very experience of living that is valued. In this context, even our work can be potentially joy-filled. Joy knits together all of our life into one seamless fabric.

GOOD MEDICINE FOR THE BODY, MIND, AND SPIRIT

The difference between joy and happiness is a subtle but important one. Happiness is often viewed as an emotional end point, something that can be attained and maintained. We've all heard comments like these:

- I will be happy when I get that big promotion.
- My life won't really be complete until I find the person of my dreams.
- Every time I see my neighbor's shiny new car, I feel unhappy with my car — even though mine is perfectly fine.

Yes, you might be happy when you reach certain milestones, but for how long? In truth, these outcomes or end points are actually way stations leading somewhere else. The outcomes we cling to are not really final, but often we equate them with a feeling state — as if that, too, will never change! Unfortunately, the attempt either to avoid a negative feeling or to grab onto a positive emotion is short-lived because it's dependent on something external — something outside of us that we can't control.

What *can* we control? We can control where we place our attention and how we regulate ourselves. This is where happiness and joy part ways. The origin of the word *joy* stems from the word meaning "to rejoice," which is all about how one plays and celebrates. While happiness is often measured by looking at various aspects of well-being and life satisfaction — some governments measure GNH, or Gross National Happiness, using factors such as health, time use, living standards, education, social vitality, and so on — joy is an uplifting, fleeting, moment-to-moment experience.

Happiness is a noun, whereas rejoicing is an action, a verb. Rejoicing is about participation in this moment. This begs the questions, How do you like to play? When was the last time you vigorously, without censorship, rejoiced and played?

Laughing is a good example of rejoicing in the moment. Scientists have found that laughter does more than lift our moods. In the 1960s, Norman Cousins researched the value of laughter for physical health — first for his own health when he was confronted with a life-threatening illness. Cousins was told he only had six months to live, and his pain was so acute that he couldn't sleep. Desperate to get some rest, he tried something that no one thought would help: a massive dose of laughter.

Cousins had a 35mm movie projector brought into his hospital room, and he projected funny films onto one wall. He soon discovered that thirty minutes of belly laughter provided him with up to two hours of anesthetic-free, pain-free sleep. (Later research supported this early claim.) This led to Cousins's recovery and, ultimately, to his working at UCLA. Today, the Cousins Center for Psychoneuroimmunology continues to do groundbreaking work exploring the mind-body connection.

At the time Cousins applied laughter as a treatment, he didn't understand how toxic stress hormones were being scrubbed from his system — or how his immune system was getting a powerful boost. Since that time, hundreds of clinical, peer-reviewed studies have demonstrated how the process works. One study, published in *Alternative Therapies in Health and Medicine*, investigated the effects of a humorous video on cancer patients. One group of cancer patients viewed the humorous video, while the control group watched a nonhumorous tourism video.

Researchers found a significant decrease in stress hormone levels for those who saw the humorous video. That matters because the stress hormone cortisol dampens the body's defense system and even kills natural killer, or NK, cells. NK cells are immune cells that fight viruses and even some kinds of tumors. The cancer group that watched the humorous video actually benefited from a significant *increase* in NK cell activity. Finding this, the researchers concluded, "As low NK cell activity is linked to decreased disease resistance and increased morbidity in persons with cancer and HIV disease, laughter may be a useful cognitive-behavioral intervention."

Laughter has also been shown to increase the levels of human growth hormone and pain-reducing endorphins. No wonder laughter feels so good. It also bonds us with others and is a social way of playing and rejoicing. Laughter and other forms of joy are effective at overcoming negative emotions. For example, have you ever been joyful and angry at the same time? Have you ever felt grateful and been envious at the same time? These are incompatible feelings. You can't feel gratitude for someone while at the same time feeling jealous or envious.

✦

Just as rumination and negative clutter can block joy, so too can joy block negative clutter. An example of this was Alina, a bright, engaging, energetic, twenty-three-year-old woman who came to see me when she experienced the return of obsessive thoughts about food and body image — and feared a relapse of her eating disorder. Fortunately, she hadn't yet started restricting food or strenuously overexercising. Having previously worked as a senior mental health therapist at the same clinic where Alina had spent three months, I knew how insidious and difficult it can be to overcome disorders such as anorexia or bulimia. Even the slightest stress can trigger the need to control food.

Alina was then under stress due to living back at home, where her mother was watching her eating habits like a hawk. Even her boyfriend had taken on a caregiver role, in which he wanted to make sure she didn't get sick again. Instead of relishing her newfound freedom from obsessive, eating-related behaviors, she found herself tense and felt as if everyone was monitoring her eating habits — which they were, of course. Initially, accepting that she was in a transitional period helped her to accept her situation a little more.

But what really helped Alina was focusing on joy. I got some clues about how she located joy during my first intake session with her. She shared that on a recent trip to New Orleans, she experienced no problems with trying different foods or spontaneously going into restaurants without first scrutinizing the menu — things she could never do when actively practicing her eating-disorder symptoms. An avid sketch artist, Alina drew loads of sketches of New Orleans's French Quarter, Bourbon Street, the Garden District, and other landmarks. When I asked Alina to bring in her sketches, she happily shared them with me. Clearly, when she focused on what truly brought her joy, she turned her attention away from the old clutter thoughts of her eating disorder.

So I gave Alina an unusual homework assignment. I asked her to imagine her hometown of Portland as an exotic city that she could capture through her sketchpad. Being a visual learner, Alina instantly took to this idea. Whenever she was noticing any eating-disorder thoughts creeping back into her head, she was instructed to take out her sketchpad and draw something beautiful or unusual. When she returned the next week, she was back in recovery mode. She was thoroughly enjoying using visual art to access joy and passion, and as a result the eating disorder thoughts had subsided.

Eating disorders are complex, and I don't tell this story to suggest that joy could be used as a stand-alone intervention for someone suffering from a full-blown, active eating disorder. For one thing, the cognitive deficits resulting from lack of proper food and nutrition could render the concept of joy incomprehensible. Still, the fact that joy could help someone struggling with obsessive thoughts is a testament to the strength and empowering impact of this de-cluttering practice.

LIFESTYLE TOOL: Daily Snapshots of Joy

These three Lifestyle Tools will help you home in on finding joy. Once you begin noticing joy in the course of your day, these practices will become more and more frequent — without your even trying. Even during those times when you might previously have found yourself irritated or annoyed, you'll find yourself looking around to take a snapshot of joy instead. How marvelous!

Experiment with the following practices to see what helps you to take those daily snapshots of joy.

1. Reflect on Gratitude

One useful way to find joy is through noticing gratitude or appreciating the things in your life. This is surprisingly easy to do. Gratitude very much depends on where you place your attention. You have a choice: you can either focus on what is missing in your life, or you can focus on what is present. Here are three types of gratitude to reflect on:

Daily Basic and Personal Gifts

Roof over your head	Transportation	Sleep
Sunlight	Health	Smiling
Running water	Furniture	Chairs
Food	Coffee/tea	Trees
Walking	Your five senses	Electricity
A job	Clothing	Silence

Daily Relationship Gifts

Friends	Family	Caregivers
Conversation	Kindness	Giving
Receiving	Closeness	Laughter
Colleagues	Supporters	Sharing
Spiritual friends	Pets	Compassion
Celebrations	Shared meals	Cooperation

Daily Paradoxical Gifts

Appreciating a "paradoxical gift" means feeling joy or gratitude for something you wish wasn't in your life. For example, if you came down with a cold or flu that kept you from going into the office, you could feel gratitude for how it forced you to slow down, think about taking better care of yourself, and get some much-needed sleep. Someone in a workshop said she was paradoxically grateful for losing her wallet because so many people were kind and helpful to her as a result of the incident. One client I worked with was paradoxically grateful for the relationship loss of her best friend because it forced her to go out and meet new people — and she met a new best friend with whom she had more in common. Paradoxical gratitude illustrates that life is not an either-or proposition. As a wise sage once said, "Pray for what you already have in your life, and you'll never be disappointed."

To practice this, think about situations in your life right now that are difficult, and use your Teflon thinking to see if you can find the bright, silver lining. What paradoxical gratitude or joy is waiting for you?

2. Find a Joy Quote That Speaks to You

For some, being inspired by words and those we admire can help us find snapshots of joy. Use one of the quotes below — or find one of your own — that inspires you to take snapshots of joy.

Carry your joy quote with you — in your purse, wallet, or smart-phone — so you can look at it throughout the day and get centered on joy. Here are a few quotes to get you started:

It is the history of our kindnesses that alone makes this world tolerable. If it were not for that, for the effect of kind words, kind looks, kind letters...I should be inclined to think our life a practical jest in the worst possible spirit.

— Robert Louis Stevenson

Enjoy, enjoy, for life is given to us, only, moment by moment.

— Richard Kirsten Daiensai

I believe that a simple and unassuming manner of life is best for everyone, best both for the body and the mind.

— Albert Einstein

Have nothing in your house that you do not know to be useful, or believe to be beautiful.

— William Morris

The world is mud-luscious and puddle-wonderful.

— e. e. cummings

3. The GLAD Snapshot Practice

GLAD is an acronym I developed for finding joy and balance. It works by paying attention to certain positive aspects of life that are around us all the time, but which frequently go unnoticed. Sound easy? It is. The acronym stands for gratitude, learning, accomplishment, and delight. Each represents a joy snapshot that you can take.

To practice this daily, use your phone or an index card at the end of the day to write down and save your GLAD experiences. Share these with others, and at the end of the week, reflect on how many joy snapshots you found.

- **Gratitude**: Take a snapshot of something you're thankful for today. This can represent any of the three types of gratitude mentioned above.
- **Learning**: Take a snapshot of something you learned about yourself today, such as noticing an insight or wisdom that you possess. It could mean having a Teflon-like attitude so that you can discover something new and interesting about another, or it could be learning a new fact or gaining a new perspective that brings joy, simply because it is fun to be curious.
- **Accomplishment**: Take a snapshot of something you accomplished today, even if it was only a tiny step forward on a long-term goal. We mistakenly believe that accomplishments have to be supersized, but some of the best accomplishments are ordinary acts of self-care or giving to another.
- **Delight**: Take a snapshot of anything that made you laugh, smile, or feel joy today. This can be a thing of beauty, a chirping bird, a flower, a funny joke, a smile, your favorite color, and so on.

✦

Which of these joy practices resonates with you the most?

Anytime you can share your joy practice with another, or ask someone what brings them joy or gratitude, you are creating a circle of joy in your life. What are some ways that you might use these practices with your family or friends?

∞

Chapter 20

NOW IS THE BEST TIME
TO CONNECT WITH PURPOSE

The secret of success is constancy to purpose.

— Benjamin Disraeli

Purpose is like the alchemist's elixir. With purpose comes the power to transform the most ordinary of actions into gold. By aligning with purpose, everything in life becomes a little shinier, more alive, more exciting, and more meaningful. Like a powerful solvent, purpose dissolves away emotional clutter. Purpose puts a luster on this moment and sharpens our ability to act with clarity and wisdom. Those with a clear purpose can usually identify specific goals that enhance their lives with a strong sense of direction and worth.

Purpose has a beginning point, a place from which we can begin to examine it, access it, and understand its depth. Connecting with purpose can be seen as a four-step process. Step one begins with examining the role that purpose has played in our life. It's helpful to honestly review how we have or haven't used purpose and values in the past. To that end, ask yourself the following:

> Looking back over my life, how have I strayed from, or lacked clarity with, my values and purpose in ways that caused hurt or suffering to others, intentionally or unintentionally?

This question is not intended to bring sorrow or make you feel badly by creating more emotional clutter. On the contrary, it's an opportunity for remorse, which is the second step toward making a course correction so you can get back on the path toward health and healing. Remorse is not a bad thing, and it's not the same as guilt. Guilt means blaming yourself needlessly over something that cannot be changed. Remorse harnesses feelings you have about your past actions in order to motivate you to act differently in the future. Through remorse you move in a new purposeful direction — rather than flagellate yourself without making any real changes. While guilt dwells in the attic of old clutter, remorse is the red light on a traffic signal — reminding you to stop and forgive yourself before moving forward when the light changes to green.

Forgiveness, then, is the third step of connecting with purpose. Forgiveness asks us to wipe the slate clean and start anew. This is not to suggest that you simply forget, but that you forgive while still remembering. Forgiving yourself for hurts you may have caused others — or forgiving others for the hurts they may have caused you — is a powerful gift to oneself. It can be helpful to take the sage advice of Nelson Mandela, who wrote, "Thinking too well of people often allows them to be better than they otherwise would."

If you can forgive and think well of others, why not also think the best of yourself? Remember, no one is perfect. If you find it hard to forgive yourself, start by accepting the truth of how difficult it is to be human, to live inside of a human body and mind, and to survive the hardships and challenges that humans face. As explored earlier, this knowledge of suffering can lead to compassion and loving-kindness for yourself and others. Anyone can have the best of intentions and still make mistakes. How wonderful that we are not all machines and that we can learn from our errors. This is what gives us resilience and hope — and leads us to the fourth step, finding the goals that align with purpose. Since purpose is the stuff that heroes are made of, it's worth taking a moment to ask: What kind of hero am I? What is my hero's purpose?

Don't be shy in answering this. Have you ever stopped to consider that you are the hero in your own life story? This perspective is the key element in applying what is often referred to as the mythical or archetypal hero's journey to one's own life. This, in turn, bestows upon each of us a special gift to share with others — our true purpose and passion.

FINDING PURPOSE THROUGH YOUR HERO'S JOURNEY

The archetypal hero's journey was thoroughly investigated by mythologist, philosopher, and writer Joseph Campbell. Basically, our hero's journey is defined by the struggles we face. It's a calling that we must all undertake, even if unwillingly. For modern examples, we can turn to popular movies, which often feature an unlikely hero who overcomes steep odds to bring justice to the world. In *The Verdict*, Paul Newman played a broken-down, alcoholic lawyer who needs something to believe in again. In the *Star Wars* films, the young and naïve Luke Skywalker is forced to face his fears and trust in the Force. In *Norma Rae*, Sally Fields played a single mom and textile worker who rallies against all odds to unionize the mill where she toils. Every hero has a purpose.

The story of the purpose-driven hero resonates with us, even as children. Think of your favorite children's book. Likely, the main character faces obstacles and grows through the experience. In fact, any transition that takes you into new life territory can be viewed as a hero's journey. Whenever you move to a new city, take a new job, end or begin a relationship, or confront a health issue, you take the hero's journey in a very real sense.

Have you ever resisted taking your journey? That's not uncommon because the journey takes us into the unknown. This reminds me of Lori, a thirty-five-year-old patient in the eating disorder clinic where I once worked. Lori had neglected to take the necessary steps to prepare for her discharge — which meant making appointments with an outside support team. We were worried about discharging her without her first having a structure of support in place.

It just so happened that on Lori's last day at the clinic, I spent a group session describing the hero's journey — even drawing a sketch of the journey on the big whiteboard in the group room. When I finished, Lori nearly leaped out of her chair with excitement. She raised her hand and exclaimed, "I know what I have to do now to start my recovery journey! I have to call up a therapist and make an appointment." The hero's journey gave Lori a clear road map. She even discovered her purpose in that moment: to actively participate in taking care of herself. Happily, she answered the call.

How many hero-type journeys do we take in a lifetime? Personally, I've taken the hero's journey more times than I can remember — and each time (hopefully) I gained new skills and levels of mindfulness. Maybe I'm a slow learner, or maybe that's just the nature of this lifelong journey of awakening and sweeping away clutter. Even reading a book such as this one can be viewed as a hero's journey. The point is that heroes are not just mythical or fictional characters. The hero is that person you look at in the mirror each morning. Here are a few examples of the ordinary heroes I've been fortunate and grateful to meet in my own life:

- The former substance user who became a drug and alcohol counselor: Her purpose was to help others heal from the wisdom gained during her own struggles.
- The former gymnast who became a coach: His purpose was to give back and help others gain from the many lessons he learned about teamwork and athletics.
- The single mom who selflessly devoted herself to her daughter: Her purpose was to give her child the opportunity to thrive and grow despite not having a father's presence or support.
- All the families I've known that have faced mental health issues: Their purpose was to find wholeness and health so that they could share their story of healing and/or volunteer to help others (through organizations like the National Alliance on Mental Illness).
- The tough motorcyclist who suffered abuse as a child: His purpose was to support and protect children from child abuse by volunteering with Bikers Against Child Abuse International.
- The women and men who face chronic pain: Their purpose was to demonstrate their incredible courage to others and to find joy and spiritual meaning despite physical limitations.
- The woman who overcame her husband's alcoholism and abuse: Her purpose was to gain independence and join a group where others could benefit from her experience.

Below, I outline the various stages of the archetypal hero's journey. As you read through them, reflect on a journey that you are currently taking or one that you are being asked to embark upon. Remember, too, that there are relationship journeys, workplace and career journeys, parenting journeys, and so on. Even if you are taking more than one journey simultaneously, choose the one that is most meaningful for you right now.

- The hero receives a call to undertake a journey or adventure, one that will require personal growth.
- The hero seeks help from, or is approached by, a wise person, mentor, or teacher who encourages the hero to follow the call.
- The hero departs on the journey, crossing the threshold from the familiar to the unfamiliar, from the ordinary world to the extraordinary, the unknown, and the mysterious. In real-world terms, this might mean entering treatment, therapy, or a recovery program.
- The hero undergoes one or more trials, during which the hero encounters allies and enemies and is tested. These trials act as initiations into greater maturity, during which the hero must recommit to the journey.
- The hero enters the deepest cave and endures the supreme ordeal. This challenge involves facing one's greatest doubts, often symbolized as the dark night of the soul.
- The hero seizes the sword that allows him or her to overcome the greatest challenge and successfully complete the journey. The "sword" can be anything, such as the mindfulness and de-cluttering Lifestyle Tools in this book.
- The hero crosses the threshold back to the ordinary world from which she or he originally came.

- The hero returns home. Transformed deeply by the experience, the hero shares this new knowledge and wisdom, which is a treasure and benefit to those in the ordinary world.

Transformation is what makes the journey so special. The hero comes back deeply changed — with a new set of values and beliefs. This translates into a whole new clarity of purpose and an understanding of how to interact in a meaningful and effective way in the "ordinary" world of daily life. While everyone's purpose is unique to his or her personal journey, there is a common approach to finding that purpose. As Joseph Campbell famously said, "Follow your bliss."

Now, having reflected on your personal journey, ask yourself the following questions. Whether you happen to be at the beginning, middle, or end of your journey, that's okay. Go as far as you can with these questions. You can still connect with purpose.

- At what place am I along the journey?
- If I have not yet embarked on my journey, what is holding me back?
- How can I find support and resources as I move through the journey?
- How do I show my commitment to taking this journey?
- What skills or tools will help me to successfully complete the journey?
- If I have completed my journey, what wisdom and purpose did I find?
- How does my journey provide me with greater clarity about my very unique and special purpose?
- Even if the journey is not complete, what purpose and values could I align with, even now, that would help me to move toward completion?

PURPOSE IS THE GIFT WE GIVE

Don't be fooled into believing your purpose has to be gargantuan or bigger than life or world-changing to be worthwhile. As written by the sixth-century Buddhist master Shantideva:

All suffering in the world results from seeking one's own happiness.
All happiness in the world results from seeking the happiness of others.

Science has even tested the timeless wisdom of giving and demonstrated that even a small, directive purpose on behalf of others can help you to live longer — and even benefit your brain. A study published in the *Journal of Gerontology: Medical Sciences* investigated how purpose — volunteering to help young children — affected older adults (with a mean age of sixty-eight) who were at risk for cognitive impairment. Researchers randomly divided participants into two groups. The first was enrolled in a community-based program called the Experience Corps, while the control group continued with a sedentary lifestyle. Both groups underwent a number of cognitive tests before and after the study, including functional magnetic resonance imaging (fMRI) to measure brain activity. Those enrolled in the Experience Corps taught and guided elementary schoolchildren in literacy, library support, and conflict resolution for fifteen hours a week. Compared to their sedentary counterparts, those who worked as tutors showed significant improvement on the cognitive tests, as well as positive changes in brain function. Researchers concluded, "These pilot results provide proof of concept for use-dependent brain plasticity in later life, and that interventions designed to promote health and function through everyday activity may enhance plasticity in key regions that support executive function." In other words, this study demonstrates the power of bringing purpose to others.

What about a more narrowly focused purpose — for example, having a reason for exercising? Exercise researcher William Morgan wondered whether "purposeful physical activity" would increase adherence to an exercise program, and he published his research in the journal *Quest*. Morgan found that, among those he studied, adding purpose led to 100 percent adherence to an exercise program. Thus, instead of just pointlessly churning away on an elliptical machine or treadmill, we help ourselves when we integrate physical activity with something meaningful — such as taking our dog or pet for a walk, walking or biking to work, or laying down a stone path to beautify the garden in our backyard. De-cluttering and finding balance by engaging with purpose can happen in a lot of different ways — through connection with others or by inviting purpose into your everyday activities and experiences.

LIFESTYLE TOOL: Purpose Is Partnership, Partnership Is Purpose

Suppose you step out the door for a simple walk around the block. You may think this is a solitary activity, but look more deeply. Taking that walk places you squarely in relationship with many things: the clothes and shoes you wear; the weather; the natural environment; neighbors; walkers, joggers, and bicyclists; cars and trucks; the sounds you encounter; pets and animals; the streets and paths of your neighborhood, and so on. You even have a relationship to the thoughts you have as you take that walk. This is true with anything you do, such as reading this paragraph. Even as I write this, I am experiencing a relationship with you, the reader.

Whatever you are doing, the bigger questions to ask yourself are these:

- How can I create healing and compassionate partnerships in my life?
- What is the purpose of the various partnerships in my life at this time?
- How can my partnerships with others be cosupportive of our mutual life goals?
- How can I create a sustainable web of partnerships and life purpose that benefits future generations?
- How can I share in the purpose of others — as they share in mine — so that all our dreams of purpose can be realized?

Write down one small, realistic goal related to purpose that you can achieve today — such as bringing a smile to another through a kind comment, doing your job to the best of your ability, being attentive as others speak, or doing something kind for yourself as a form of self-compassion and self-care.

Next, write down one specific, long-term gift of purpose that is meaningful for you — something that you can offer to one or more persons in the next week. This might mean spending supportive time with a grandchild, child, friend, or family member. It could be volunteering at the local food bank or other nonprofit organization. It could be creating a community-based group to reduce suffering. It could be sharing the story of your journey and what you've learned with another.

Anytime you can share your purpose with another, or ask someone what gives her or him a sense of purpose, you create a circle of purpose in your life.

CLOSURE IS THE NEW BEGINNING

Just as with the hero's journey, I like to think of every book ending as the call to a new beginning. Every voyage brings us full circle, looking back at how far we've come and wondering what's next. In closing, here is a *Clearing Emotional Clutter* blessing you can use along this path:

May I find my strengths each day.
May I be the one who moves my own elevator.
May I open my heart and mind to others,
letting me hear the music of all tribes.
May I find abiding peace
and relief from suffering and clutter of all kinds.
And may I compassionately assist all beings
on the clutter-free path of fidelity to this moment,
while living with purpose, simplicity, and joy.

∞

ACKNOWLEDGMENTS

My deepest gratitude extends to all those individuals who have dedicated themselves to sharing teachings of peace and mindfulness with others. I thank my late teacher, Venerable U Silananda, who was a dedicated mindfulness guide for many years; Ashin Thitzana, a spiritual friend and monk brother who inspires many with his knowledge and dedication; U Thondara and the monks and community of the Burma Buddhist Monastery; Randy Fitzgerald, a friend and talented writer whose generous sharing of ideas and enthusiasm always planted seeds of hope and optimism; Greg Crosby, Jeff Horacek, Heather Nielsen, John Barnes, and other friends who offered suggestions and shared ideas in this book's early formative period; former and present board members of The Center for Mindful Eating, for reducing suffering through an enlightened awareness of food and eating; Georgia Hughes, editorial director, who offered many wonderful ideas and who willingly and patiently traveled the journey of discovery as we developed this book; the New World Library publishing family — Kristen Cashman, Munro Magruder, Kim Corbin, Ami Parkerson, Tona Pearce Myers, freelance copyeditor Jeff Campbell, and others — for bringing a depth of insights, dedication, and experience to the project. This acknowledgment would not be complete without mentioning Publisher Marc Allen, who has been true to his mission of manifesting "books that change lives."

I am grateful for the friends, colleagues, guides, clients, acquaintances, and students who have joined me on the path of awakening. I am also deeply indebted to my father, Norman, and especially my mother, Barbara, who always had an encouraging word and continues to support my spiritual and creative interests.

Finally, I extend deepest thanks to Maria Brignola, dance movement therapist and teacher, whose ideas and feedback were invaluable. Maria, thank you for sharing joy, light, love, and meaning. You are my Princess Monk and *Bak'u del cuore*.

NOTES

INTRODUCTION

Page 1, *"Don't own so much clutter"*: Wendell Berry, *Farming: A Hand Book* (Berkeley, CA: Counterpoint Press, 2011), 67.

Page 8, *Researchers from Harvard, in a study published in* Science: Matthew Killingsworth and Daniel Gilbert, "A Wandering Mind Is an Unhappy Mind," *Science* 330, no. 6006 (2010): 932.

Page 10, *As songwriter Leonard Cohen once wrote, "Well, my friends"*: Leonard Cohen, "Tower of Song," http://lyrics.wikia.com/wiki/Leonard_Cohen:Tower_Of _Song (accessed July 13, 2015).

CHAPTER 1: STOP RIDING THE EMOTIONAL ELEVATOR

Page 15, *"Help me to love a slow progression"*: Gunilla Norris, *Being Home: Discovering the Spiritual in the Everyday* (Mahwah, NJ: HiddenSpring Books, 1991), 16.

Page 17, *In fact, a study conducted by psychologists at the University of Virginia*: Timothy Wilson, et al., "Just Think: The Challenges of the Disengaged Mind," *Science* 345, no. 6192 (2014): 75–77.

Page 17, *To verify our mind's ability to scare the hell out of us, researchers tested*: Adam Radomsky, et al., "You Can Run but You Can't Hide: Intrusive Thoughts on Six Continents," *Journal of Obsessive-Compulsive and Related Disorders* 3, no. 3 (2014): 269–79.

Page 18, *"I had an experience at a young age"*: Paul Harrison, phone interview on April 11, 2015.

CHAPTER 2: INNER-FACEBOOKING

Page 23, *"What if you could erase everybody's memory"*: John Nelson, *Matrix of the Gods* (Norfolk, VA: Hampton Roads Publishing Company, 1994), 9–10.

Page 24, *In one of the biggest studies of its kind in the United Kingdom*: Peter Kinderman, et al., "Psychological Processes Mediate the Impact of Familial Risk, Social Circumstances and Life Events on Mental Health," *PLoS ONE* 8, no. 10 (October 2013).

Page 25, *As Professor Peter Kinderman, lead researcher of the UK study*: University of Liverpool, "Dwelling on Negative Events Biggest Cause of Stress," October 17, 2013, http://news.liv.ac.uk/2013/10/17/dwelling-on-negative -events-biggest-cause-of-stress/ (accessed December 10, 2014).

Page 25, *Dr. Jeffrey Schwartz, author of* Brain Lock, *is a pioneer in neuroplasticity*: Jeffrey Schwartz, *Brain Lock* (New York: Harper Perennial, 1996).

Page 27, *J. David Creswell published research in* Psychosomatic Medicine *that*: J. David Creswell, et al., "Neural Correlates of Dispositional Mindfulness during Affect Labeling," *Psychosomatic Medicine* 69, no. 6 (2007): 560–65.

CHAPTER 3: CULTIVATE A BEAUTIFUL
GARDEN OF THOUGHT

Page 33, *"The flowers of positive experiences crowd out"*: Rick Hanson, *Hardwiring Happiness: The New Brain Science of Contentment, Calm, and Confidence* (New York: Harmony Books, 2013), 125.

Page 33, *Buddhist teacher Lama Surya Das, a true* wise guy: Lama Surya Das, *Words of Wisdom* (Kihei, HI: Koa Books, 2008), 30.

CHAPTER 4: THE PEACE OF ACCEPTANCE

Page 43, *"We can rent our grievances the master bedroom"*: Fred Luskin, *Forgive for Good* (New York: HarperOne, 2003), 8.

Page 44, *In* Think on These Things, *world teacher and author Krishnamurti*: Jiddu Krishnamurti, *Think on These Things* (New York: HarperOne, 1964/1989), 123.

Page 46, *A study published in the* American Journal of Psychiatry: Martin Teicher, et al., "Hurtful Words: Association of Exposure to Peer Verbal Abuse with Elevated Psychiatric Symptom Scores and Corpus Callosum Abnormalities," *American Journal of Psychiatry* 167, no. 12 (December 2010): 1464–71.

CHAPTER 5: GET CENTERED IN YOUR BREATH AND BODY

Page 55, *"You see, consciousness thinks it's running the shop"*: Joseph Campbell, with Bill Moyers, *The Power of Myth* (New York: Anchor Books, 1991), 181.

Page 58, *A study in* Cognitive Therapy and Research Journal *found that*: Jan M. Burg and Johannes Michalak, "The Healthy Quality of Mindful Breathing: Associations with Rumination and Depression," *Cognitive Therapy and Research Journal* 35, no. 2 (April 2011): 179–85.

Page 58, *Meanwhile, a study published in* Clinical Psychological Science *showed*: Elissa Epel, et al., "Wandering Minds and Aging Cells," *Clinical Psychological Science* 1, no. 1 (2013): 75–83.

Page 62, *You'll also be following the advice of Henry David Thoreau*: Henry David Thoreau, www.goodreads.com/quotes/50588-you-must-live-in-the-present -launch-yourself-on-every (accessed December 27, 2014).

CHAPTER 6: CLEANSING FAMILY EMOTIONAL CLUTTER

Page 65, *"To survive the time in the woods, your old"*: Julie Tallard Johnson, *Wheel of Initiation: Practices for Releasing Your Inner Light* (Rochester, VT: Bear & Company, 2010), 2–3.

Page 67, *Epigenetics may hold the key to making the sage advice from Einstein*: Albert Einstein, www.goodreads.com/quotes/4464-peace-cannot-be-kept-by-force -it-can-only-be (accessed January 25, 2015).

Page 67, *Research at Duke University, conducted by scientist Randy Jirtle*: Randy Jirtle and Michael Skinner, "Environmental Epigenomics and Disease Susceptibility," *Nature Reviews Genetics* 8 (April 2007): 253–62.

Page 68, *In* The Science of the Art of Psychotherapy, *child development researcher*: Allan Schore, *The Science of the Art of Psychotherapy* (New York: W. W. Norton & Company, 2012), 441.

Page 71, *"Do not look for bad company"*: Thomas Byrom, trans., *Dhammapada: The Sayings of the Buddha* (Boston: Shambhala, 1976/1993), 23.

CHAPTER 7: REFLECTIONS
ON COMPASSIONATE COMMUNICATION

Page 77, *"Compassion, in Tibetan terms, is a spontaneous feeling"*: Yongey Mingyur Rinpoche, *The Joy of Living: Unlocking the Secret and Science of Happiness* (New York: Three Rivers Press, 2007), 105.

Page 77, *story written in 1885 by Russian novelist Leo Tolstoy called "Three Questions"*: Leo Tolstoy, *What Men Live By and Other Tales* (1918; repr., Rockville, MD: Wildside Press, 2009).

Page 82, *In* Attachment in Adulthood, *researchers Mario Mikulincer and Phillip Shaver*: Mario Mikulincer and Phillip Shaver, *Attachment in Adulthood: Structure, Dynamics, and Change* (New York: Guilford Press, 2010).

Page 82, *A study published in the* Journal of Personality and Social Psychology: Mario Mikulincer, et al., "Attachment, Caregiving, and Altruism: Boosting Attachment Security Increases Compassion and Helping," *Journal of Personality and Social Psychology* 89, no. 5 (2005): 817–39.

CHAPTER 8: PLANTING FRIENDSHIP SEEDS

Page 87, *"Remember, the path is never as arduous as it looks"*: Frank Coppieters, *Handbook for the Evolving Heart* (Marina del Rey, CA: CONFLU:X Press, 2006), 145.

Page 88, *A large meta-analytic review looked at 148 different studies*: J. Holt-Lunstad, et al., "Social Relationships and Mortality Risk: A Meta-analytic Review," *Public Library of Science Medicine* 7, no. 7 (2010).

Page 88, *A study conducted in Australia, published in the* Journal: Lynne Giles, et al., "Effect of Social Networks on 10 Years Survival in Very Old Australians: The Australian Longitudinal Study of Aging," *Journal of Epidemiology and Community Health* 59 (2005): 574–79.

Page 89, *In the first study to investigate how emotions like happiness*: James H. Fowler and Nicholas A. Christakis, "The Dynamic Spread of Happiness in a Large Social Network: Longitudinal Analysis Over 20 Years in the Framingham Heart Study," *British Medical Journal* 337, no. a2338 (2008): 1–9.

Page 95, *As the wise sage and poet Rumi reminds us*: Rumi, www.goodreads.com /quotes/20338-people-want-you-to-be-happy-don-t-keep-serving-them (accessed November 5, 2014).

CHAPTER 9: FOR THE LOVE OF LISTENING

Page 97, *"You can talk and talk, but the longer you talk"*: Glenn Clark, *The Man Who Talks with the Flowers: The Intimate Life Story of Dr. George Washington Carver* (Shakopee, MN: Macalester Park Publishing, 1939/1994), 45.

Page 98, *Published in the* Proceedings of the National Academy of Sciences: Diana I. Tamir and Jason P. Mitchell, "Disclosing Information About the Self Is Intrinsically Rewarding," *Proceedings of the National Academy of Sciences of the United States of America* 109, no. 21 (May 2012): 8038–43.

Page 101, *"If you want to become full, let yourself be empty"*: Lao Tzu, *Tao Te Ching*, trans. Stephen Mitchell (New York: Harper Perennial, 2006), 22.

CHAPTER 10: EXPANDING YOUR TRIBE

Page 107, *"A human being is a part of the whole, called by us"*: Albert Einstein, https://en.wikiquote.org/wiki/Albert_Einstein (accessed October 12, 2014).

Page 110, *"See yourself in others. Then whom can you hurt?"*: Byrom, *Dhammapada*, 36.

Page 111, *"People have difficulty"*: David Bohm, *On Dialogue* (London: Routledge Classics, 1996/2004), 8–9.

Page 113, *A study published in* Psychological Science *found*: Isaac Smith, et al., "The Moral Ties That Bind…Even to Out-Groups: The Interactive Effect of Moral Identity and the Binding Moral Foundations," *Psychological Science* 25, no. 8 (June 2014): 1554–62.

Page 113, *"If you are a poet, you will see clearly that there"*: Thich Nhat Hanh, *The Heart of Understanding: Commentaries on the Prajnaparamita Heart Sutra* (Berkeley, CA: Parallax Press, 1988/2009), 3–4.

CHAPTER 11: CHANGE THE DISTRACTION
CHANNEL TO FIND CLARITY

Page 117, *"A child born today is practically never away from the"*: Robert Johnson and Jerry Ruhl, *Contentment: A Way to True Happiness* (New York: HarperCollins, 1999), 104–5.

Page 117, *"When gamblers play," explained Schull in an interview*: Alice Robb, "Why Are Slot Machines so Addictive?" *New Republic*, December 5, 2013, www.newrepublic.com/article/115838/gambling-addiction-why-are-slot -machines-so-addictive (accessed November 28, 2014)

Page 118, *The latter task force found that exposure to pervasive sexualizing*: American Psychological Association, "Report of the APA Taskforce on the Sexualization of Girls," www.apa.org/pi/women/programs/girls/report-full.pdf (accessed January 23, 2015).

Page 122, *In* The Mindful Brain, *psychiatrist Daniel Siegel wrote*: Daniel Siegel, *The Mindful Brain* (New York: W. W. Norton & Company, 2007), 177.

Page 124, *Author Deepak Chopra defined intention this way*: Deepak Chopra, *The Spontaneous Fulfillment of Desire: Harnessing the Infinite Power of Coincidence* (New York: Harmony, 2004), 209.

Page 125, *Brain researcher Benjamin Libet, author of* Mind Time, *studied this ability*: Benjamin Libet, *Mind Time: The Temporal Factor in Consciousness* (Cambridge, MA: Harvard University Press, 2005), 141.

CHAPTER 12: VACCINATE YOURSELF AGAINST AFFLUENZA

Page 129, *"Wisps of steam rise from the kettle"*: Soshitsu Sen XV, *Tea Life, Tea Mind* (New York: Weatherhill, 1995), 29.

Page 131, *In their book* Affluenza, *authors John de Graaf*: John de Graaf, David Wann, and Thomas Naylor, *Affluenza: The All-Consuming Epidemic* (San Francisco: Berrett-Koehler Publishers, 2005), 2.

Page 133, *Mother Teresa eloquently spoke of this in her poem "True Drops of Love"*: Mother Teresa, JourneyofHearts.org, www.journeyofhearts.org/kirstimd/saint .htm (accessed December 9, 2014).

Page 134, *A study published in* Psychological Science *titled "A 'Present' for the Future"*: Ting Zhang, et al., "A 'Present' for the Future: The Unexpected Value of Rediscovery," *Psychological Science* (August 2014), doi: 10.1177/0956797614542274.

CHAPTER 13: PUT THE BRAKES ON WORK AND SPEED

Page 141, *His research, published in the* Journal of Cross-Cultural Psychology: Robert Levine and Ara Norenzayan, "The Pace of Life in 31 Countries," *Journal of Cross-Cultural Psychology* 30, no. 2 (March 1999): 178–205.

Page 146, *"The path of freedom/Does not lead"*: Inayat Khan, *The Gayan: Notes from the Unstruck Music* (Tucson: Message Publications, 1985), 78.

Page 146, *"The mother doesn't simply let the child"*: Ajahn Amaro, *Finding the Missing Peace* (Hemel Hempstead, U.K.: Amaravati Publications, 2011), 96.

Page 148, *author John O'Donohue, who wrote, "Your body is the only home"*: John O'Donohue, *Anam Cara: A Book of Celtic Wisdom* (New York: HarperCollins, 1998).

CHAPTER 14: NATURE'S CLEANSING POWER OF HOPE

Page 151, *"Negativity is totally unnatural. It is a psychic pollutant"*: Eckhart Tolle, *The Power of Now: A Guide to Spiritual Enlightenment* (Novato, CA: New World Library, 1999/2004), 189.

Page 152, *"Hope is both the earliest and the most indispensable virtue"*: Erik Erikson, www.goodreads.com/quotes/193624-hope-is-both-the-earliest-and-the-most -indispensable-virtue (accessed September 9, 2015).

Page 157, *A study published in the journal* Computers in Human Behavior: Yalda Uhls, et al., "Five Days at Outdoor Education Camp without Screens Improves Preteen Skills with Nonverbal Emotion Cues," *Computers in Human Behavior* 39 (October 2014): 387–92.

CHAPTER 15: DAILY FLEXIBILITY, SOFTENING, AND LETTING BE

Page 163, *"Use the Teflon side of your mind"*: Surya Das, *Words of Wisdom*, 79.

Page 165, *"At the age of eight, I was given a rifle and taken hunting"*: Randy Fitzgerald, phone interview on June 11, 2015.

Page 167, *In* Mindfulness, *Langer concluded, "The regular and 'irreversible' cycles"*: Ellen Langer, *Mindfulness* (Boston: Da Capo Press, 1989), 112–13.

Page 169, *A study published in the journal* Proceedings of the National: Melissa Rosenkranz, et al., "Affective Style and *In Vivo* Immune Response: Neuro-behavioral Mechanisms," *Proceedings of the National Academy of Sciences of the United States* 100, no. 19 (September 2003), doi: 10.1073/pnas.1534743100: 11148–52.

Page 170, *Richard Davidson, one of the study's researchers, concluded*: Emily Carlson, "Study Shows Brain Activity Influences Immune Function," *Eureka Alert!*, September 1, 2003, www.eurekalert.org/pub_releases/2003-09/uow-ssb082903 .php (accessed December 27, 2014).

Page 170, *He wrote, "If you affirm 'I am well,' but think"*: Paramahansa Yogananda, *Scientific Healing Affirmations* (Los Angeles: SRF Publications, 1990), 15.

CHAPTER 16: AWAKEN THE COMPASSIONATE HEART TODAY

Page 177, *"The best and most beautiful things in the world"*: Helen Keller,
The Story of My Life (Garden City, NJ: Doubleday, Page & Company,
1921), 203.

Page 178, *In* Just One Thing, *neuropsychologist Rick Hanson wrote, "The brain"*.
Rick Hanson, *Just One Thing: Developing a Buddha Brain One Simple Practice
at a Time* (Oakland, CA: New Harbinger Publications, 2011), 217.

Page 179, *"The weak can never forgive"*: Mahatma Gandhi, www.brainyquote
.com/quotes/quotes/m/mahatmagan121411.html (accessed January 28, 2015).

Page 180, *A study published in the* Journal of Personality and Social Psychology:
Barbara Fredrickson, et al., "Open Hearts Build Lives: Positive Emotions,
Induced through Loving-Kindness Meditation, Build Consequential
Personal Resources," *Journal of Personality and Social Psychology* 95, no. 5
(November 2008): 1045–62.

Page 180, *In another study, a team of researchers at the Duke University Medical
Center*: James Carson, et al., "Loving-Kindness Meditation for Chronic Low
Back Pain: Results from a Pilot Trial," *Journal of Holistic Nursing* 23, no. 3
(September 2005): 287–304.

CHAPTER 17: FIDELITY TO THE MOMENT

Page 187, *"To be truly alive is to feel one's ultimate existence"*: Christian Wiman, *My
Bright Abyss: Meditation of a Modern Believer* (New York: Farrar, Straus, and
Giroux, 2014), 92.

Page 187, *authors Robert Johnson and Jerry Ruhl consider this to mean "a vow of
fidelity"*: Johnson and Ruhl, *Contentment*, 85.

Page 190, *Of his research findings, he wrote, "The Amish are faring pretty well"*: Robert
Biswas-Diener, "4 Ways to Start Simplifying Your Life," *Psychology Today*,
August 20, 2014, www.psychologytoday.com/blog/significant-results
/201408/4-ways-start-simplifying-your-life.

CHAPTER 18: BECOME A MASTER
AT UNTYING KNOTS EACH MOMENT

Page 195, *"If you want to untie a knot, you must first find"*: Lama Govinda, *The Lost
Teachings of Lama Govinda: Living Wisdom from a Modern Tibetan Master*, ed.
Richard Power (Wheaton, IL: Quest Books, 2007), 85.

Page 196, *As Zen master Bernie Glassman said in* The Dude and the Zen Master: Jeff
Bridges and Bernie Glassman, *The Dude and The Zen Master* (New York: Blue
Rider Press, 2012), 222.

Page 198, *A study published in the journal* Appetite *investigated food cravings*: H. J.
Alberts, et al., "Coping with Food Cravings: Investigating the Potential of a
Mindfulness-Based Intervention," *Appetite* 55, no. 1 (August 2010): 160–63.

CHAPTER 19: TAKE DAILY SNAPSHOTS OF JOY

Page 205, *"Be content with what you have, rejoice in the way things are"*: Diane Durston, *Wabi Sabi: The Art of Everyday Life* (North Adams, MA: Storey Publishing, 2006), 113.

Page 208, *One study, published in* Alternative Therapies in Health and Medicine: Mary Bennett, et al., "The Effect of Mirthful Laughter on Stress and Natural Killer Cell Activity," *Alternative Therapies in Health and Medicine* 9, no. 2 (2003): 38–45.

Page 213, *"It is the history of our kindnesses that alone"*: Kay Redfield Jamison, *An Unquiet Mind* (New York: Vintage Books, 1995), 146.

Page 213, *"Enjoy, enjoy, for life is given to us, only"*: Richard Kirsten Daiensai, *Smile: 365 Happy Meditations* (London: MQ Publications, 2004), 201.

Page 213, *"I believe that a simple and unassuming manner of life"*: Durston, *Wabi Sabi*, 115.

Page 213, *"Have nothing in your house that you do not know"*: Durston, *Wabi Sabi*, 112.

Page 213, *"The world is mud-luscious and puddle-wonderful"*: Durston, *Wabi Sabi*, 212.

CHAPTER 20: NOW IS THE BEST TIME
TO CONNECT WITH PURPOSE

Page 215, *"The secret of success is constancy to purpose"*: John Baldoni, *Lead with Purpose: Giving Your Organization a Reason to Believe in Itself* (New York: Amacom, 2012), 122.

Page 216, *It can be helpful to take the sage advice of Nelson Mandela, who wrote*: Baldoni, *Lead with Purpose*, 25.

Page 222, *"All suffering in the world results from seeking"*: Shantideva, www.meditation -research.org.uk/well-being/ (accessed January 28, 2015).

Page 222, *A study published in the* Journal of Gerontology: Michelle Carlson, et al., "Evidence for Neurocognitive Plasticity in At-Risk Older Adults: The Experience Corps Program," *Journal of Gerontology: Medical Sciences* 64, no. 12 (December 2009): 1275–82.

Page 223, *Exercise researcher William Morgan wondered whether "purposeful"*: William Morgan, "Prescription of Physical Activity: A Paradigm Shift," *Quest* 53, no. 3 (2001): 366–82.

Bibliography

Altman, Donald. *101 Mindful Ways to Build Resilience: Tools for Calm, Clarity, Optimism, and Happiness*. Eau Claire, WI: PESI Publishing and Media, 2015.

———. *Art of the Inner Meal: The Power of Mindful Practices to Heal Our Food Cravings*. Portland, OR: Moon Lake Media, 2002.

———. *The Joy Compass: 8 Ways to Find Lasting Happiness, Gratitude and Optimism in the Present Moment*. Oakland, CA: New Harbinger Publications, 2012.

———. *Living Kindness: The Buddha's Ten Guiding Principles for a Blessed Life*. Portland, OR: Moon Lake Media, 2003.

———. *Meal by Meal: 365 Daily Meditations for Finding Balance with Mindful Eating*. Novato, CA: New World Library, 2004.

———. *The Mindfulness Code: Keys for Overcoming Stress, Anxiety, Fear, and Unhappiness*. Novato, CA: New World Library, 2010.

———. *The Mindfulness Toolbox: 50 Practical Tips, Tools, & Handouts for Anxiety, Depression, Pain, and Stress*. Eau Claire, WI: PESI Publishing and Media, 2014.

———. *One-Minute Mindfulness: 50 Simple Ways to Find Peace, Clarity, and New Possibilities in a Stressed-Out World.* Novato, CA: New World Library, 2011.

Amaro, Ajahn. *Finding the Missing Peace.* Hemel Hempstead, UK: Amaravati Publications, 2011.

Arden, John. *Brain2Brain: Enacting Client Change through the Persuasive Power of Neuroscience.* Hoboken, NJ: John Wiley & Sons, 2015.

———. *Rewire Your Brain: Think Your Way to a Better Life.* Hoboken, NJ: John Wiley & Sons, 2010.

Baldoni, John. *Great Communication Secrets of Great Leaders.* New York: McGraw-Hill, 2003.

———. *Lead by Example: 50 Ways Great Leaders Inspire Results.* New York: Amacom, 2009.

———. *Lead with Purpose: Giving Your Organization a Reason to Believe in Itself.* New York: Amacom, 2012.

———. *MOXIE: The Secret to Bold and Gutsy Leadership.* Brookline, MA: Bibliomotion, 2014.

Beattie, Melody. *Gratitude: Affirming the Good Things in Life.* New York: Ballantine, 1992.

Biswas-Diener, Robert, and Todd Kashdan. *The Upside of Your Dark Side: Why Being Your Whole Self — Not Just Your "Good" Self — Drives Success and Fulfillment.* New York: Hudson Street Press, 2014.

Bohm, David. *On Dialogue.* London and New York: Routledge, 1996.

Bridges, Jeff, and Bernie Glassman. *The Dude and the Zen Master.* New York: Blue Rider Press, 2012.

Buber, Martin. *I and Thou.* New York: Scribner, 1970.

Byrom, Thomas, trans. *Dhammapada: The Sayings of the Buddha.* Boston: Shambhala, 1993.

Campbell, Joseph, with Bill Moyers. *The Power of Myth.* New York: Anchor Books, 1991.

Chödrön, Pema. *Start Where You Are: A Guide to Compassionate Living.* Boston: Shambhala, 1994/2004.

Chopra, Deepak. *The Spontaneous Fulfillment of Desire: Harnessing the Infinite Power of Coincidence.* New York: Three Rivers Press, 2003.

Church, Dawson. *The Genie in Your Genes: Epigenetic Medicine and the New Biology of Intention.* Fulton, CA: Elite Books, 2009.

Clark, Glenn. *The Man Who Talks with the Flowers: The Life Story of Dr. George Washington Carver.* St. Paul, MN: Macalester Park Publishing, 1994.

Clement, Brian. *LifeForce: Superior Health and Longevity.* Summertown, TN: Healthy Living Publications, 2007.

Coppieters, Frank. *Handbook for the Evolving Heart.* Marina del Rey, CA: CONFLU:X Press, 2006.

Davidson, Richard, and Sharon Begley. *The Emotional Life of Your Brain.* New York: Plume, 2012.

de Graaf, John, David Wann, and Thomas Naylor. *Affluenza: The All-Consuming Epidemic.* San Francisco: Berrett-Koehler Publishers, 2005.

de Mello, Anthony. *Awareness: The Perils and Opportunities of Reality.* New York: Image Books, 1992.

Durston, Diane. *Wabi Sabi: The Art of Everyday Life.* North Adams, MA: Storey Publishing, 2006.

Easwaran, Eknath. *The Mantram Handbook: Formulas for Transformation.* Petaluma, CA: Nilgiri Press, 1977.

Frankl, Viktor. *Man's Search for Meaning.* Boston: Beacon Press, 2006.

Gandhi, Mahatma. *The Way to God: Selected Writings from Mahatma Gandhi.* Edited by M. S. Deshpande. Berkeley, CA: North Atlantic Books, 2009.

Gargiulo, Terrence. *Once upon a Time: Using Story-Based Activities to Develop Breakthrough Communication Skills.* San Francisco: Pfeiffer, 2007.

Govinda, Lama. *The Lost Teachings of Lama Govinda: Living Wisdom from a Modern Tibetan Master.* Edited by Richard Power. Wheaton, IL: Quest Books, 2007.

Gunaratana, Bhante Henepola. *Eight Mindful Steps to Happiness: Walking the Buddha's Path.* Somerville, MA: Wisdom Publications, 2001.

Hanson, Rick. *Buddha's Brain: The Practical Neuroscience of Happiness, Love & Wisdom.* Oakland, CA: New Harbinger, 2009.

———. *Hardwiring Happiness: The New Brain Science of Contentment, Calm, and Confidence.* New York: Harmony Books, 2013.

———. *Just One Thing: Developing a Buddha Brain One Simple Practice at a Time.* Oakland, CA: New Harbinger, 2011.

Johnson, Robert, and Jerry Ruhl. *Contentment: A Way to True Happiness.* New York: HarperCollins, 1999.

Keating, Thomas. *Open Mind, Open Heart: The Contemplative Dimension of the Gospel.* New York: Continuum, 1997.

Khan, Inayat. *Notes from the Unstruck Music from the Gayan of Inayat Khan.* Tucson, AZ: Message Publications, 1985.

Kirsten Daiensai, Richard. *Smile: 365 Happy Meditations.* London: MQ Publications, 2004.

Krishnamurti, Jiddu. *Think on These Things.* New York: HarperOne, 1989.

Langer, Ellen. *Mindfulness.* Boston: Da Capo, 1989.

Lao Tzu. *Tao Te Ching.* Translated by Stephen Mitchell. New York: Harper Perennial, 1990.

Libet, Benjamin. *Mind Time: The Temporal Factor in Consciousness.* Cambridge, MA: Harvard University Press, 2005.

Lind-Kyle, Patt. *Heal Your Mind, Rewire Your Brain: Applying the Exciting New Science of Brain Synchrony for Creativity, Peace, and Presence.* Santa Rosa, CA: Energy Psychology Press, 2009.

Linley, Alex, Janet Willars, and Robert Biswas-Diener. *The Strengths Book: Be Confident, Be Successful, and Enjoy Better Relationships by Realising the Best of You.* Coventry, UK: CAPP Press, 2010.

Luskin, Fred. *Forgive for Good.* New York: HarperOne, 2003.

Mahasi, Sayadaw. *Fundamentals of Vipassana Meditation.* Berkeley, CA: Dhammachakka Meditation Center, 1991.

Maitreya, Ananda, trans. *The Dhammapada.* Berkeley, CA: Parallax Press, 1995.

Mehl-Madrona, Lewis. *Healing the Mind through the Power of Story: The Promise of Narrative Psychiatry.* Rochester, VT: Bear & Company, 2010.

Mikulincer, Mario, and Phillip Shaver. *Attachment in Adulthood: Structure, Dynamics, and Change.* New York: Guilford Press, 2010.

Nhat Hanh, Thich. *The Heart of Understanding: Commentaries on the Prajna-paramita Heart Sutra*. Berkeley, CA: Parallax Press, 2009.

———. *The Miracle of Mindfulness: An Introduction to the Practice of Meditation*. Boston: Beacon, 1987.

O'Connor, Richard. *Undoing Perpetual Stress: The Missing Connection between Depression, Anxiety, and 21st Century Illness*. New York: Berkley Trade, 2006.

O'Donohue, John. *Beauty: The Invisible Embrace*. New York: Harper Perennial, 2005.

———. *Eternal Echoes: Celtic Reflections on Our Yearning to Belong*. New York: Harper Perennial, 2000.

Ogburn, William Fielding. *Social Change with Respect to Culture and Original Nature*. Ithaca, NY: Cornell University Library, 1922/2009.

Ratey, John, and Eric Hagerman. *Spark: The Revolutionary New Science of Exercise and the Brain*. New York: Little, Brown and Company, 2008.

Salzberg, Sharon. *Lovingkindness: The Revolutionary Art of Happiness*. Boston: Shambhala, 1995.

Schore, Allan. *The Science of the Art of Psychotherapy*. New York: W. W. Norton & Company, 2012.

Schwartz, Jeffrey, and Sharon Begley. *The Mind and The Brain: Neuroplasticity and the Power of Mental Force*. New York: ReganBooks, 2002.

Schwartz, Jeffrey, and Rebecca Gladding. *You Are Not Your Brain: The 4-Step Solution for Changing Bad Habits, Ending Unhealthy Thinking, and Taking Control of Your Life*. New York: Avery, 2011.

Seligman, Martin. *Learned Optimism: How to Change Your Mind and Your Life*. New York: Pocket Books, 2006.

Siegel, Dan. *The Mindful Brain*. New York: W. W. Norton & Company, 2007.

Silananda, Sayadaw U. *The Four Foundations of Mindfulness*. Somerville, MA: Wisdom Publications, 1990.

Somov, Pavel. *The Lotus Effect: Shedding Suffering and Rediscovering Your Essential Self*. Oakland, CA: New Harbinger Publications, 2010.

Soshitsu Sen XV. *Tea Life, Tea Mind*. New York: Weatherhill, 1995.

Stafford, Kim. *100 Tricks Every Boy Can Do*. San Antonio, TX: Trinity University Press, 2012.

Stevenson, Robert Louis. *The Letters of Robert Louis Stevenson*. 2 vols. Fairford, UK: Echo Library, 2006.

Surya Das, Lama. *Awakening the Buddha Within: Tibetan Wisdom for the Western World*. New York: Broadway Books, 1997.

———. *Buddha Standard Time: Awakening to the Infinite Possibilities of Now*. New York: HarperOne, 2011.

———. *Words of Wisdom*. Kihei, HI: Koa Books, 2008.

Suzuki, Shunryu. *Zen Mind, Beginner's Mind*. Edited by Trudy Dixon. Boston: Shambhala, 2010.

Tallard Johnson, Julie. *Wheel of Initiation: Practices for Releasing Your Inner Light*. Rochester, VT: Bear & Company, 2010.

Tolle, Eckhart. *The Power of Now: A Guide to Spiritual Enlightenment*. Novato, CA: New World Library, 2004.

Wiman, Christian. *My Bright Abyss: Meditation of a Modern Believer*. New York: Farrar, Straus, and Giroux, 2014.

Yogananda, Paramahansa. *Scientific Healing Affirmations*. Los Angeles: SRF Publications, 1990.

Yongey, Mingyur Rinpoche. *The Joy of Living: Unlocking the Secret and Science of Happiness*. New York: Three Rivers Press, 2007.

About the Author

Donald Altman, MA, LPC, is a psychotherapist, former Buddhist monk, and award-winning author. A past vice president of The Center for Mindful Eating, he serves on the organization's advisory board. Donald is currently an adjunct professor in the Interpersonal Neurobiology program at Portland State University and has also taught at Lewis and Clark College Graduate School of Education and Counseling.

Donald conducts mindful living and mindful eating workshops and retreats internationally and has trained thousands of mental health therapists and healthcare workers on how to use mindfulness as a tool for managing depression, anxiety, pain, and stress. He is known as America's Mindfulness Coach for the way he integrates timeless mindfulness tools, neuroscience, and spiritual values into modern life. Donald trained with Venerable U Silananda, author of *The Four Foundations of Mindfulness*, at a Buddhist monastery located near the San Bernardino Mountains in Southern California. He is a member of the Burma Buddhist Monastery Association.

A prolific writer whose career spans more than thirty years, Donald has written several books, including *The Mindfulness Toolbox*, which won two 2015 national Benjamin Franklin Gold awards as the best book in the psychology and body, mind, and spirit categories, and *The Mindfulness Code*, which *Spirituality & Health* selected as "one of the best spiritual books of 2010." He has also written for an Emmy Award–winning children's television program and has had numerous articles appear in print. An avid motorcyclist, Donald enjoys riding along the Oregon coast. He lives in Portland, Oregon.

For information about Donald Altman's books, guided meditation CDs, workshops, and speaking and consulting services, visit www.MindfulPractices.com.